Big . . . Bad . .

A Farce

Philip King
and
Falkland L. Cary

Based on an idea by
Ivan Butler

Samuel French - London
New York - Toronto - Hollywood

BIG ... BAD ... MOUSE!

Presented by Michael Codron in association with A.L.S. Presentations Ltd at the Shaftesbury Theatre, London, on 17th October 1966, with the following cast of characters:

(in order of their appearance)

FIONA JONES	*Anna Carteret*
HAROLD HOPKINS	*Bunny May*
MISS SPENCER	*Elspeth Duxbury*
MR PRICE-HARGRAVES	*Jimmy Edwards*
MR BLOOME	*Eric Sykes*
LADY CHESAPEAKE	*Joan Young*
DORIS POVEY	*Clovissa Newcombe*

The play directed by ALEXANDER DORÉ

Setting by BRIAN CURRAH

SYNOPSIS OF SCENES

The action of the play passes in the Orders office of Chunkibix Limited

ACT I

SCENE 1 9 a.m. on a morning in December
SCENE 2 9 a.m. the following morning

ACT II

SCENE 1 Around midnight following evening
SCENE 2 9 a.m. the following morning

Time—the present

ACT I

Scene I

SCENE—*An office in a large block occupied by Chunkibix Ltd. Nine o'clock on a morning in early December.*

The office is a bright and cheerful place, with large windows across the back and R *walls. The main door opens up* RC *on to a small alcove, and another door down* R *leads to an inner office. A massive and imposing desk stands* LC, *and a much plainer and humbler one* R. *A small desk for a secretary is up* C, *against the wall of the alcove and with its chair back to the window. There is a hatstand up* LC, *and a filing cabinet* R *of the main door.*

When the CURTAIN *rises, the room is empty. After a moment* FIONA JONES *dashes in through the main door. She is about eighteen years old, madly modern in her attire and outlook—somewhat dumb, but very pretty. She wears a revealing blouse and skirt and carries a large, gaily-coloured bag and a duster. Immediately on her entrance she throws the duster on to Mr Bloome's desk,* R, *consults her wristlet watch and, presumably, checks with a clock on the "fourth wall". She then dives into the large bag and produces a transistor wireless set, puts it on the desk, drops the bag on the floor, and switches the set on. She then picks up her duster and begins flicking dust off the desk. As soon as the radio is switched on an* AN-NOUNCER *is heard.*

ANNOUNCER. ... that the record she has asked me to play for you will help restore you to your usual sunny self. What is the record?

FIONA. Well, what is it, for heaven's sake?

ANNOUNCER. It's none other than the—(*his voice rising*)—The Twaddlers! (*Or any contemporary pop group*)

(FIONA *gives a loud, strangled, agonized cry of ecstasy*)

The Twaddlers! In their very latest recording—"Hootah, hootah, choo, choo, choo!"

(*There is another scream from* FIONA, *and immediately a loud noise comes from the transistor—guitars, the Mersey Sound, and a nerve-racking, thumping beat.* FIONA, *with yet another wild cry, flings the duster into the air, then flings herself into a madly acrobatic, strenuous and abandoned version of "The Twaddlers", squawking loudly as she does so. Almost immediately the door up* RC *opens and* HAROLD HOPKINS *appears. He is a pale-faced, bespectacled lad of nineteen or so. He is carrying a folder filled with letters. On seeing the door open,* FIONA *stops "twisting" for the tenth of a second, but on seeing Harold her alarm vanishes and the dancing is renewed, more energetically than ever. "On-the-ball Harold" takes in the situation at once. With a blood-curdling whoop he throws the folder desk-wards. It misses the large desk and falls to the floor.* HAROLD *rushes to-wards Fiona, faces her, and immediately joins in the wild cavorting, which goes on until the record—after one chorus only—fades out and the* An-nouncer's *voice is heard again. Immediately, the dancing stops,* Harold *drops to his hands and knees quickly and begins to pick up the letters.* Fiona *switches off the transistor*)

FIONA (*squirming*) Oh, Harold, aren't they fab!

HAROLD. I say! Won't Miss Spencer be in any minute now?

FIONA. Well, get you, Harold Hopkins! Scared of old "droopy-drawers" Spencer! (*Witheringly*) Honestly, I don't know!

HAROLD (*picking up letters*) Don't know what?

FIONA. What I see in you, or why I bother about you. I mean to say—just look at you!

(HAROLD *looks at himself as much as possible*)

When I think of all the boys I know—you know, smashin' lookers—and then I have to go and fall for a drip like you!

HAROLD (*grinning*) P'raps I've got hidden charms!

FIONA. Where do you hide them? (*Quickly*) *Stop!* I don't want to know. (*Smiling at him*) Come here, Harold!

HAROLD. I must get these letters sorted before . . . (*Looking at a letter as he rises*) Cor, old Meggitts don't half splash with their enve-lopes, do they!

FIONA (*exasperated*) Oh my . . . ! (*She moves quickly to Harold and plants a fervent, lingering kiss on his lips*)

(HAROLD *tries to protest at first, then yields to Fiona's ardour. Letters slide from the folder to the floor, the folder follows them.* HAROLD *tries to disentangle himself from Fiona's embrace*)

HAROLD (*weakly*) The letters—if Miss Spencer—if Mr Price-Hargraves . . .

FIONA (*firmly*) Now you kiss me!

HAROLD. I—I—oh hell! (*He seizes* FIONA *and, bending her backwards, kisses her in what he imagines to be a "film-star" manner. It is a rather clumsy, though sincere effort*)

FIONA (*with a squeak*) Oo! My back!

(*They break away*)

(*Her hands on her back*) Ouch! (*Smiling*) Not bad, Harold, for nine o'clock in the morning.

(HAROLD *staggers almost drunkenly to the large desk, clutches it for support, and wipes his brow with a handkerchief*)

(*Brightly*) Well, now I feel ready to cope with Miss Spencer, Mr Price-Hargraves, Mr Bloome, Uncle Tom Cobleigh and all!

Harold (*weakly*) Well, I don't! (*With a yelp*) The letters! (*He totters towards them, kneels, and picks them up*)

(*The telephone on the desk* lc *rings.* Fiona *answers it*)

Fiona. Orders Department. Mr Price-Hargraves' and Mr Bloome's office . . . Miss Spencer? . . . No, she isn't in yet, but I suppose you'd better put 'em through . . . Hullo? . . . No, I'm sorry, Miss Spencer isn't in yet. Can I give her a message? (*She props a compact on the desk and uses her lipstick while she talks*) Yes, I'll tell her and that you'll ring again. 'Bye! (*She replaces the receiver*) A private call for Miss Spencer. Can you imagine the row there'd be if anybody rang *me* up here? (*Indicating the letters*) Hey! There seems to be a lot of letters this morning!

Harold (*grinning*) There are!

Fiona (*with a snort*) And I'm on my own! Maudie Arnold went home with a stinking cold last night. And I'll bet most of those— (*indicating letters*)—are for old Price-Hargraves.

Harold. What difference does that make? You type Mr Bloome's letters as well, don't you?

Fiona (*contemptuously*) He'll be lucky if he gets any done today. Price-Hargraves'll see to it his are done first. (*She moves away* r)

Harold (*putting some letters on the desk* lc) Funny chap, Bloome— the way he lets Price-Hargraves boss him around. And the way Miss Spencer treats him—as if he wasn't there.

Fiona. He isn't—as far as she's concerned, you clot! Can't you see it's Price-Hargraves is her pin-up? Harold, you're just too innocent for this world!

Harold. Innocent, me! (*He gives a low growl, grabs Fiona, and once again gives her his film-star kiss*)

(Miss Spencer *enters up* rc. *She is a thin spinster in her forties, very business-like, but very feminine in her devotion to Mr Price-Hargraves. She is in outdoor clothes, and carries a shopping bag*)

Miss Spencer (*seeing Fiona and Harold locked in embrace*) Oh!

(Fiona *and* Harold *break apart*)

(*Moving between them; horrified*) Miss Jones!!

Fiona (*in a dither*) I—good morning, Miss Spencer.

Harold (*also dithering*) Er—'morning, Miss Spencer.

Miss Spencer. Such outrageous conduct, *and* in Mr Price-Hargraves' office, *and* in the firm's time! Really—you teenagers. No sense of decency—no morals. Fling ourselves into the arms of the opposite sex on every possible occasion. (*To Harold*) Remove yourself from this office immediately. (*She puts her shopping bag on her chair up* c *and hangs her coat on the stand*)

Harold. Yes, Miss Spencer.

Miss Spencer. Have you sorted the letters out?

HAROLD. Yes, Miss Spencer. (*Putting some of the letters on the desk* R) These are Mr Blocme's.

MISS SPENCER (*with a snort*) Never mind Mr Bloome's. (*Moving above the desk* LC) Are these for Mr Price-Hargraves?

HAROLD. Yes, Miss Spencer.

MISS SPENCER. Then you may go.

HAROLD. Yes, Miss Spencer.

MISS SPENCER (*picking up a small vase with drooping flowers in it, from the desk* LC) Oh! You can throw these away for me, please, and put fresh water in the vase.

(HAROLD *takes the vase and moves to the door down* R)

Miss Jones!

HAROLD. Yes, Miss Spencer. (*Realizing his mistake*) Oh!

(HAROLD *exits down* R. FIONA *picks up her duster*)

MISS SPENCER. You have quite enough to be getting on with, Miss Jones. You know Miss Arnold won't be in today.

FIONA (*dusting*) Thank goodness for that. If you'd heard her sniffing all day yesterday—got on my nerves.

MISS SPENCER. Have you dusted the desks?

FIONA. I've done Mr Bloome's. I haven't got round to Mr Price-Hargraves' yet.

MISS SPENCER (*almost in a panic*) Not—got round to . . . ? Good heavens, girl! (*She snatches the duster and starts to give Fiona everything on the desk, dusting as she does so*)

FIONA (*plaintively*) I've only one pair of hands, Miss Spencer.

MISS SPENCER. Surely you know you should have done Mr Price-Hargraves first? These books are covered in dust. Here, hold this. (*She hands a blotter to Fiona and dusts frantically*) What on earth would he think if he came in and found his desk . . . (*She hands a letter-tray to Fiona*) And this. (*She works round* L *of the desk and below it*)

FIONA (*moving down* R *of the desk*) I don't suppose he'd notice—men never do.

MISS SPENCER (*still dusting frantically; with a tremendous sigh*) Mr Price-Hargraves is not like other men.

(MR PRICE-HARGRAVES *is heard off in the corridor—a loud and hearty voice*)

PRICE-HARGRAVES (*off; some way down the corridor*) Ah! Mornin', Tattersall.

VOICE (*off*) Morning, P.H.!

PRICE-HARGRAVES (*off, approaching*) Morning, J.D.!

MISS SPENCER (*in ecstasy*) Mr Price-Hargraves! (*She drops the duster and crawls under the knee-hole of the desk to retrieve it*)

(FIONA *drops everything back on the desk and moves below Bloome's desk* R)

VOICE (*off*) 'Morning, P.H.

PRICE-HARGRAVES (*off; heartily*) Has the Sanderson order gone off?

VOICE (*off*) Last night.

PRICE-HARGRAVES (*off*) Good show, J.D. Good show!

(PRICE-HARGRAVES *enters up* RC, *closing the door behind him. He is pompous, fiftyish, perhaps fat and bald. He wears a bowler and carries umbrella and briefcase*)

PRICE-HARGRAVES (*moving down* C, *looking unconsciously at Miss Spencer's posterior and speaking automatically*) Good show, Miss Spencer, good show!

(MISS SPENCER *straightens up swiftly and stands below the desk*)

'Mornin', Miss Spencer. 'Mornin', Miss Jones.

(HAROLD *bursts in from the door down* R *as Price-Hargraves speaks, carrying the small vase filled with water. He trips over the waste-paper basket below the desk* R, *and as he falls, throws the water over Price-Hargraves' trousers*)

HAROLD (*as he enters*) Here we are, Miss Spencer. The . . . Oh, sorry, sir!

(FIONA *picks up her bag*)

PRICE-HARGRAVES. Dammit, boy! (*Fuming*) Look at my trousers! I'm soaked!

MISS SPENCER (*wildly*) Oh, Mr Price-Hargraves!

HAROLD. I'm sorry I—I—I . . .

PRICE-HARGRAVES. Soaked!

MISS SPENCER. Oh, Mr Price-Hargraves, let me . . . (*She grabs the duster, rushes to Price-Hargraves, kneels and begins to rub his trousers vigorously*)

PRICE-HARGRAVES. Higher, Miss Spencer.

(MISS SPENCER *starts to raise the duster too high*)

Miss Spencer!

(MISS SPENCER *drops the duster.* HAROLD *starts to polish Price-Hargraves' shoes.* PRICE-HARGRAVES *holds his wet trousers away from his leg*)

(*To Hopkins*) Hopkins, leave this room! *Out!*

HAROLD. Yes, sir!

(HAROLD, *in his agitation, hands the vase to Price-Hargraves, and rushes out of the office down* R)

PRICE-HARGRAVES (*unconscious of the vase*) Has everyone gone mad this morning? (*Glaring at Fiona*) What is that girl standing there like that for? *Out!*

(FIONA *exits hurriedly down* R)

(*Realizing he is holding the vase; incensed*) What the—where did this come from?

MISS SPENCER (*almost wailing*) Oh, give it to me, Mr Price-Hargraves. I'll put it down. (*She takes the vase and puts it on the desk* LC)

(PRICE-HARGRAVES *takes blotting paper from the desk* R *and puts it down inside his trousers. All his movements are governed by the fact that he has to walk with the blotting paper inside his trouser leg*)

PRICE-HARGRAVES. I won't ask what has been going on in here. Perhaps you will enlighten me in your own good time. (*He wriggles uncomfortably*)

(MISS SPENCER *starts to speak*)

But not now, if you don't mind. (*He hangs up his hat and umbrella*) We have an extremely busy day in front of us. I see Mr Bloome hasn't arrived yet. (*Moving down* RC) Surely he is not favouring us with the pleasure of his absence for the day?

MISS SPENCER. If you remember, Mr Price-Hargraves, you suggested he call at Watkins Ltd, on his way to the office—about their invoices. (*She moves to her desk*)

PRICE-HARGRAVES. H'mm. I think I'd better get rid of an invoice myself. (*He turns his back on the audience, removes the blotting paper and throws it on Bloome's desk*) H'mm. I seem to have blotted my copy-book. (*Moving above his own desk* LC) Ah well! Work! Work! Work! "Time and tide wait for no man", do they?

MISS SPENCER (*agreeing madly*) They don't indeed.

PRICE-HARGRAVES (*gazing at his desk in horror*) *Miss* Spencer!

MISS SPENCER (*quivering*) What? What, Mr Price-Hargraves?

(PRICE-HARGRAVES *extends a hand silently and dramatically towards the chaos on his desk*)

(*With a cry of anguish*) Oh! Oh, Mr Price-Hargraves! Your desk!

PRICE-HARGRAVES (*solemnly, pompously*) My desk, Miss Spencer.

MISS SPENCER. Oh—what can I say?

PRICE-HARGRAVES. Actions speak louder than words, Miss Spencer. (*He moves majestically away to Bloome's desk*)

(MISS SPENCER, *almost in tears, begins feverishly to tidy the big desk*)

(*Surveying Bloome's desk, witheringly*) Mr Bloome's desk is in *perfect* order, not a thing out of place. (*Almost pained*) I find that a little hard to bear, Miss Spencer, seeing that I do happen to be the senior occupant of this office. Perhaps Mr Bloome possesses some—er—endearing quality which I lack, though I cannot imagine what that could be! (*He stands humming pompously*)

(MISS SPENCER *takes a bunch of flowers quickly from the shopping bag, thrusts them into the vase and puts them on the desk* LC)

MISS SPENCER. Your desk is ready now, Mr Price-Hargraves.

PRICE-HARGRAVES (*with a frosty smile*) Better late than never, eh, Miss Spencer? Now perhaps we really *can* get down to some work. (*He sits at his desk*)

(MISS SPENCER *moves to her own desk*)

(*Holding up the pile of letters in a fan shape*) Quite a—er (*smiling fatuously*) a *fan* mail this morning, Miss Spencer. (*He beams at her, pleased with his joke*)

MISS SPENCER (*blankly*) Can't I deal with some of the letters for you?

PRICE-HARGRAVES. No, no! You know my golden rule. (*Very pompously*) When one has been chosen to hold a responsible position one should accept full responsibility. Our chairman, Lady Chesapeake, has honoured me with great responsibility. She feels I . . .

MISS SPENCER. I'm sure she values you enormously.

PRICE-HARGRAVES (*with relish*) She thinks I am a pearl of great price—Hargraves. (*He laughs again at his own joke*)

(MISS SPENCER, *after a blank moment, joins in*)

MISS SPENCER. Can't I . . . ?

PRICE-HARGRAVES. You can deal with Mr Bloome's. I'm sure his will be all rubbish.

MISS SPENCER (*unhappily*) Yes, Mr Price-Hargraves. (*She crosses to Bloome's desk and sits*)

(PRICE-HARGRAVES *briefly peruses each letter. As he does so he mumbles, starting, "Dear Chunkibix . . .". He puts one letter in the "Out" tray, another in the "In" tray, hesitates on the third and finally screws it up and throws it in the waste-paper basket. As he does so, his telephone rings*)

(*Leaping up*) Oh, shall I take it, Mr . . .

PRICE-HARGRAVES (*waving her away and lifting the receiver, speaking his hyphened name with relish*) This is Price-Hargraves here . . . Who? . . . Miss Spencer? . . . *Who* wishes to speak to her? (*Not too pleased*) A private call for you, Miss Spencer.

MISS SPENCER. Oh, Mr Price-Hargraves—not during office hours —they can't—they shouldn't . . .

PRICE-HARGRAVES. They *have*. (*Into the phone; coldly*) Put this call through to Mr Bloome's desk, will you? (*He gestures grandly to Miss Spencer*)

MISS SPENCER (*gibbering*) Oh, but Mr Price-Hargraves—I don't know that I ought to take the call. It isn't right—during working hours. I—I . . . (*She lifts the receiver at Bloome's desk, waiting for the call*)

PRICE-HARGRAVES. Oh, take the call! Shall I leave the room?

MISS SPENCER. Oh, no, not unless you need to—(*confused*)—*want* to, I mean.

PRICE-HARGRAVES (*coldly*) I don't.

MISS SPENCER (*into the phone*) Hullo, who's that? . . . Doris? (*To Price-Hargraves*) My niece. Doris, what on earth are you doing,

ringing me up at the office? . . . Upset, why? What's happened? . . .
What! . . . Oh, no, no, no, no!

PRICE-HARGRAVES. Good news, Miss Spencer?

MISS SPENCER. Oh, Mr Price-Hargraves, I think I'm going to
faint.

PRICE-HARGRAVES. If you faint none of us will know what has
happened. What *has* happened? (*He rises*)

MISS SPENCER. My niece has been attacked by a man! (*Into the
phone*) Doris, where did it happen? . . . Wandsworth Common? (*To
Price-Hargraves*) Wandsworth Common.

PRICE-HARGRAVES. Wandsworth Common.

MISS SPENCER. Poor Doris! The brute didn't actually . . . ?

PRICE-HARGRAVES (*hurrying to Bloome's desk; eagerly*) Well, did he?

MISS SPENCER. You're sure about that? (*To Price-Hargraves*) She
always was a good runner.

(BLOOME *enters up* RC. *He is a neat little man, about forty, with an
occasional nervous twitch. He carries an umbrella and briefcase, and wears
a bowler. He stands just inside the door, behind Price-Hargraves*)

Oh, the brute, the beast, the devil, the monster!

BLOOME (*coughing nervously*) Is that Mr Watkins about the invoices?

PRICE-HARGRAVES. No, it is not!

(BLOOME *hangs up his hat and umbrella on the stand*)

MISS SPENCER (*holding the receiver in her hand as she reports the conversation*) He chased her.

PRICE-HARGRAVES. Good heavens!

MISS SPENCER. Across the common.

PRICE-HARGRAVES. Great Scott!

(FIONA *enters down* R)

FIONA. 'Morning, Mr Bloome.

PRICE-HARGRAVES. *Out!*

(FIONA *runs off down* R. BLOOME *moves* L *of Price-Hargraves, takes a
paper from his briefcase and hands it to him*)

BLOOME. The report on the Watkin invoices . . .

PRICE-HARGRAVES. Blast the Watkins invoices! (*He grabs the
paper and throws it in the waste-paper basket. To Miss Spencer*) Did he
catch her?

MISS SPENCER (*on the phone*) Did he catch you?

BLOOME. If I may interrupt . . .

(PRICE-HARGRAVES *snatches Bloome's briefcase and throws it on the
floor above the desk.* BLOOME *crosses above him and kneels on the floor
above the end of the desk to pick up his case*)

PRICE-HARGRAVES. *Did he catch her?*

MISS SPENCER (*on the phone*) Oh, good!

PRICE-HARGRAVES (*delightedly*) He *did* catch her!

MISS SPENCER (*into the phone*) That's what I'd do if it happened to me . . . I know, dear, but once sex raises it's ugly head . . .

(*At this precise moment, Bloome's head appears above the end of the desk, as he rises*)

No, dear, you can't come here.

(BLOOME *moves* L *of Price-Hargraves*)

PRICE-HARGRAVES. Of course she can.

MISS SPENCER (*into the phone*) Of course you can.

PRICE-HARGRAVES. Tell her she can pick you up here as soon as she likes.

MISS SPENCER (*into the phone*) You can pick me up here as soon as you likes.

PRICE-HARGRAVES. Tell her she can tell *me* all about it.

MISS SPENCER (*into the phone*) You can tell *me* all about it.

(PRICE-HARGRAVES *looks at her angrily.* MISS SPENCER *replaces the receiver.* PRICE-HARGRAVES *turns to Bloome*)

PRICE-HARGRAVES (*looking at his watch*) You're late.

BLOOME (*fiddling with his briefcase zip; nervously*) But—but—but . . .

PRICE-HARGRAVES. Same old excuse. And don't fiddle with your zip. (*He moves above Bloome to his own desk and sits*)

BLOOME (*moving up stage; to Miss Spencer*) May I have a word about the Watkins invoices?

MISS SPENCER. There ought to be a law against them!

BLOOME. Invoices?

MISS SPENCER. No. Men.

BLOOME (*surprised*) A law against Mr Price-Hargraves?

MISS SPENCER (*rising quickly and rushing below the desk towards Price-Hargraves; almost whimpering*) Oh, no! Mr Price-Hargraves is not a man!

PRICE-HARGRAVES. Eh?

MISS SPENCER (*standing* R *of Price-Hargraves*) I mean—not just an ordinary one.

(BLOOME *slips quickly into his chair*)

Oh, Mr Price-Hargraves, I hope you didn't think I meant—oh, Mr Price-Hargraves, I couldn't bear it if you thought I meant . . .

PRICE-HARGRAVES (*beaming*) Of course not, Miss Spencer, of course not. Though of course (*with a glance at Bloome*) I really *am* the only man in the office.

MISS SPENCER. Yes, yes!

BLOOME. No, no! And, Miss Spencer, may I have the Watkins invoices?

MISS SPENCER (*disregarding Bloome*) Terrible! Terrible! My sister's daughter attacked last night.

PRICE-HARGRAVES (*murmuring*) Oh, Miss Spencer!

MISS SPENCER. On Wandsworth Common.

PRICE-HARGRAVES (*shocked*) Oh, Miss Spencer!

MISS SPENCER. Chased right across it without so much as a by-your-leave!

PRICE-HARGRAVES. Oh, Miss Spencer!

MISS SPENCER. Ooooh! I'd just like to have five minutes alone with the man who did it!

BLOOME. Oh, Miss Spencer!

(MISS SPENCER *and* PRICE-HARGRAVES *glare at Bloome, then turn away*)

And if I could have the remaining Watkins in . . .

PRICE-HARGRAVES. Damn the Watkins invoices! You saw the Watkins people this morning, didn't you?

BLOOME. Yes, I did.

PRICE-HARGRAVES. Well, I hope you gave them hell—about the errors they'd made.

BLOOME. Hell? Well—er—no, not exactly.

PRICE-HARGRAVES. But dammit, man, you had the argument—the facts to put before them.

BLOOME. Oh, yes, I had the argument, and the facts. Unfortunately I hadn't the invoices.

PRICE-HARGRAVES. What!

BLOOME. Miss Spencer hadn't put them in my briefcase.

MISS SPENCER (*furious*) What?

BLOOME (*to Price-Hargraves*) I asked her to put them in my case last night.

MISS SPENCER. No, no!

BLOOME. Yes, yes. Then just as she was getting them, she was called away about something very important, naturally.

MISS SPENCER. Yes, yes!

BLOOME. No—er, yes. And, er, I suppose the invoices were forgotten.

PRICE-HARGRAVES (*angrily*) Bloome! Kindly stop making excuses for yourself! It is your business to ensure you have the necessary papers with you when you make calls on behalf of the firm. Your responsibility and no-one else's.

BLOOME. I'm sorry, Mr Price-Hargraves. Of course it was my fault.

PRICE-HARGRAVES. There are too many of such faults, Mr Bloome. (*He turns again to his work*)

(MISS SPENCER *sits at her desk and busies herself.* HAROLD *enters down* R)

HAROLD. 'Scuse me, Mr Price-Hargraves, but . . .

PRICE-HARGRAVES (*in a roar*) *Out!*

(HAROLD *runs out up* RC. *The telephone on the desk* LC *rings*. BLOOME *indicates this*)

I am aware for whom the bell tolls, Bloome. (*He answers the phone*) Price-Hargraves! . . . (*To Bloome, agitatedly*) It's the chairman!

(BLOOME *and* PRICE-HARGRAVES *both rise. Throughout the conversation, they both bow each time Lady Chesapeake is mentioned by name.* BLOOME *does an extra one just before they sit*)

Good morning, Lady Chesapeake . . . Yes, Lady Chesapeake . . . But, of course, Lady Chesapeake . . . I'd be delighted, Lady Chesapeake. (*He replaces the receiver*) That was Lady Chesapeake. (*He sits*)

(BLOOME *gives an extra bow, and sits*)

She's on her way here. She wants to know how the arrangements are going for the staff party tomorrow night. They are complete, I presume?

BLOOME. I have arranged everything—the paper hats, the whisky, the balloons . . .

PRICE-HARGRAVES. I sincerely hope you have. I didn't like having to leave things entirely in your hands, but if you can assure me . . .

BLOOME. I can, I can . . .

PRICE-HARGRAVES. To work, to work! Let us all set an example— shoulders to the grindstone, noses to the wheel. (*Shouting*) Miss Jones! Miss Jones!

(FIONA *runs in*)

FIONA. Yes, sir?

PRICE-HARGRAVES. Dictation! Get your pad and pencil!

FIONA. Yes, sir!

(FIONA *runs out*)

PRICE-HARGRAVES. Now, Miss Spencer—toil, toil, toil. (*Shouting*) Hopkins! Hopkins!

(HOPKINS *runs in up* RC)

HAROLD. Yes, sir?

PRICE-HARGRAVES. Toil, toil, toil!

(BLOOME *picks up a pencil to make notes*)

HAROLD. I beg your pardon, sir?

PRICE-HARGRAVES. Don't just stand there. Toil! Look alive—do something.

HAROLD. What do you want done, sir?

PRICE-HARGRAVES. Anything! Sharpen a pencil.

(HAROLD *snatches Bloome's pencil and grinds at it on the sharpener at the filing cabinet up* R. FIONA *rushes in with her pad and pencil.* PRICE-HARGRAVES *paces the office.* FIONA *clashes with him on her way to sit* R *of his desk. Everyone looks very busy)*

PRICE-HARGRAVES. Right, Miss Jones, take a memo to all personnel of the Orders Department . . .

FIONA. That's us!

PRICE-HARGRAVES. Don't interrupt. (*He approaches Bloome's desk*) To whom it may concern . . . (*He sees the transistor*) Good Heavens, Bloome, what's this?

BLOOME. I don't know, I . . .

PRICE-HARGRAVES. It's not a piece of office equipment. Get rid of it! Lady Chesapeake mustn't see that!

BLOOME. But . . .

(HAROLD *shoves the pencil back in Bloome's hand*)

PRICE-HARGRAVES. At once. (*He moves down* L)

(FIONA *signals to Bloome that the set is hers*)

BLOOME. Yes, sir. (*He shrugs and drops the set into the waste-paper basket down* R *of his desk*)

(*Immediately the radio blares out full blast with a "rhythm group".* PRICE-HARGRAVES *gives a gurgling yelp and splutters, waving his arms about.* FIONA *starts to gyrate to the music.* MISS SPENCER *rushes to Price-Hargraves and starts slapping his back.* HAROLD *sits on Bloome's desk and starts conducting with a pencil. The door up* RC *opens and* LADY CHESAPEAKE, *a large, formidable, tweedy person of around fifty, sails through the doorway*)

LADY CHESAPEAKE (*topping everything*) What is going on in here? (*She moves down* C)

(BLOOME *sits on the basket to muffle the radio, then takes it out and bangs it on his desk. It stops playing. There is a deadly silence as* LADY CHESAPEAKE *turns her glance on everyone in turn*)

LADY CHESAPEAKE (*with chilling audibility*) The offices of Chunkibix Limited turned into a palais de dance!

BLOOME. No, no, it . . .

LADY CHESAPEAKE (*turning on Bloome*) And *you—you*, Mr Bloome, leader of the band!

BLOOME (*coughing nervously*) I—oh—I . . .

MISS SPENCER (*frantically*) Lady Chesapeake, you don't understand; it . . .

LADY CHESAPEAKE (*to Miss Spencer*) A moment later, and I suppose I would have found *you* doing the can-can.

MISS SPENCER (*agonized*) My lady . . .

LADY CHESAPEAKE. Or perhaps strip-tease is your speciality? (*Looking at her*) No—I should think—*not!*

PRICE-HARGRAVES. May I—may I try to explain?

LADY CHESAPEAKE. You may not. That this should take place and that you should permit it!

PRICE-HARGRAVES. But I . . .

LADY CHESAPEAKE. Unworthy—ignoble—despicable!

BLOOME. Lady Chesapeake, I've got to explain.

LADY CHESAPEAKE. Mr Bloome, up to one moment ago you were employed in a responsible position in the Order Department. But you have changed Orders into *Dis*orders. And whether your services will be further required depends on your future behaviour. Now, you will repeat after me: "In the firm of Chunkibix we do not tolerate moral looseness." Come on.

BLOOME. We do not tolerate moral looseness.

LADY CHESAPEAKE. Or careless work.

BLOOME. Or careless work.

LADY CHESAPEAKE. Or avoidable errors.

BLOOME. Or avoidable errors.

LADY CHESAPEAKE. Now get back to your work!

BLOOME. Now get back to your work!

LADY CHESAPEAKE. Mr Bloome, I will see you later!

(BLOOME *nervously bangs the radio on his desk and it blares forth again. He snatches it up and runs across* L *below Price-Hargraves, throwing the set to the latter as he passes.* PRICE-HARGRAVES *juggles with it, trying to muffle it, and finally bangs it on his own desk. It stops.* BLOOME *hides behind Price-Hargraves*)

(*In the same flat, deadly voice*) Miss Spencer! Pad and pencil—get them.

PRICE-HARGRAVES. Might I suggest . . .

LADY CHESAPEAKE (*instantly*) You might not.

(*There is silence for a moment*)

I am waiting, Miss Spencer.

MISS SPENCER (*leaping to Lady Chesapeake, pad and pencil in hand*) Ready, Lady . . .

LADY CHESAPEAKE. Take this down—head it "Warning".

MISS SPENCER (*surprised*) I beg your pardon?

LADY CHESAPEAKE (*witheringly*) I said: "Warning." Am I going too fast for you, Miss Spencer?

MISS SPENCER (*wincing*) No, Lady Chesa . . .

LADY CHESAPEAKE (*dictating*) To all employees *and all* executives. (*She glances coldly towards Bloome and Price-Hargraves*)

(BLOOME, *under her gaze, eases his collar*)

(*Dictating*) In future, no employees will bring any musical instruments into the works or offices. Any employee found to be in possession of radios, televisions, concertinas, mouth-organs, brass instruments or woodwind, will be liable to instant dismissal. Have you got that, Miss Spencer?

MISS SPENCER. Yes, Lady Chesapeake.

LADY CHESAPEAKE. Copies to be posted on all notice-boards in the building. (*She glances round at them*) You will all hear more of this later.

(LADY CHESAPEAKE *exits up* RC. HAROLD *and* FIONA *exit down* R. PRICE-HARGRAVES *looks tragically at Miss Spencer.* MISS SPENCER *returns the gaze. After a moment* BLOOME *starts tip-toeing across to his desk*)

PRICE-HARGRAVES (*whispering*) Bloome . . .

BLOOME (*turning below his desk; in almost a squeak*) Yes?

PRICE-HARGRAVES. You have ruined us all.

BLOOME. Yes.

PRICE-HARGRAVES. You have ruined yourself—me . . .

BLOOME. Yes.

PRICE-HARGRAVES. You have ruined Miss Spencer.

BLOOME. No! (*Correcting himself*) Yes.

PRICE-HARGRAVES. What is there left?

BLOOME (*wildly*) The Watkins in—voi—(*correcting himself*)—nothing.

PRICE-HARGRAVES. Aspirins, Miss Spencer. *Aspirins!*

(MISS SPENCER *nods—unable to speak*)

I—I need them. A lot of aspirins.

MISS SPENCER (*opening her bag and looking in*) Oh!

PRICE-HARGRAVES. What?

MISS SPENCER. There aren't any. I'll . . .

PRICE-HARGRAVES. No, no. Let me drain the cup. No future—no aspirins!

BLOOME. Mr Price-Hargraves . . .

PRICE-HARGRAVES (*ignoring him*) Perhaps cyanide would be better.

MISS SPENCER. Oh, no, no!

PRICE-HARGRAVES. Oh, yes, yes!

BLOOME. Mr Price-Hargraves . . .

PRICE-HARGRAVES. Work goes on, Miss Spencer. The letters. (*He moves* L *of his desk and sits at it*)

(MISS SPENCER *sits at her desk*).

BLOOME (*urgently*) Mr Price-Hargraves!

PRICE-HARGRAVES. I am trying to pretend you are not there, Bloome. What is it?

BLOOME. I would like to leave the room.

(PRICE-HARGRAVES *looks at Bloome with a heavy eye.* BLOOME *raises his hand, schoolboy fashion*)

PRICE-HARGRAVES (*looking away from him; with a faint wave of the hand and in a faint voice*) Out!

(BLOOME *moves uncertainly to the door up* RC *and exits*)

(*Looking at his hands*) With these two hands I could strangle him. (*He rises and moves below his desk to* R, *pacing*)

MISS SPENCER (*wildly*) But the mischief's done, Mr Price-Hargraves. Strangling Mr Bloome wouldn't do any good.

PRICE-HARGRAVES. It would do Mr Bloome a lot of good.

MISS SPENCER (*in anguish*) Mr Price-Hargraves, please—please don't pace. Please try to rest.

PRICE-HARGRAVES (*with scorn*) Rest! No, I must pace.

MISS SPENCER. You'll wear yourself out. Please, do sit.

PRICE-HARGRAVES. I shall never sit down again. What would be the use of sitting down? I couldn't concentrate on anything. (*With a broad gesture towards his desk*) On anything.

MISS SPENCER. No, no, of course you couldn't. But it might help.

PRICE-HARGRAVES (*with a wail*) If I could get Lady Chesapeake's icy eyes out of my mind.

MISS SPENCER. And her icy mouth! Oh! (*She rises*) Do you mind if I pace too? (*She paces behind Price-Hargraves*)

PRICE-HARGRAVES (*unheeding*) And what she said! What she said! Those cruel words!

MISS SPENCER (*whimpering*) Unworthy . . .

PRICE-HARGRAVES. Ignoble . . .

MISS SPENCER (*with a howl*) Despicable . . . !

PRICE-HARGRAVES. Am I—am *I* even one of those things, Miss Spencer?

MISS SPENCER (*magnificently*) You are all three! (*Hastily*) I mean, none of the three.

PRICE-HARGRAVES (*pacing down* R) My head is spinning!

(MISS SPENCER *follows him closely*)

(*Turning and finding her close behind him*) Miss Spencer, will you kindly stop following me around. This is not the London to Brighton Walking Race!

MISS SPENCER (*hurt*) Following you around! (*She moves to her desk*) I was only . . .

(*There is a knock on the door down* R *and* FIONA *enters*)

FIONA. 'Scuse me, but . . .

PRICE-HARGRAVES (*automatically*) Out!

FIONA (*also automatically*) Yes, sir. (*She opens the door*)

PRICE-HARGRAVES. Wait! What was it you . . . ?

FIONA. I was wondering whether you would like your coffee now?

PRICE-HARGRAVES (*in a hollow voice, moving* L) I shall never want my coffee again. Out!

FIONA (*quite normally*) Very good, sir.

(FIONA *exits down* R. LADY CHESAPEAKE *enters up* RC)

LADY CHESAPEAKE. Miss Spencer, I wish to speak to Mr Price-Hargraves—alone.

(MISS SPENCER *exits hurriedly up* RC)

And now, Mr Price-Hargraves, can I ask you to tell me why you have allowed all discipline to disappear from this office?

(PRICE-HARGRAVES *tries to speak, but fails*)

(*Moving towards him below the desk* LC) You see, you can't. (*She looks at him*) Mr Price-Hargraves, I'm not entirely devoid of feeling. There is something troubling you. Something personal. Something emotional. Something causing you deep embarrassment.

(PRICE-HARGRAVES *tries again to speak*)

Come along, come along. Stop shilly-shallying. What is it you're trying to tell me?

(DORIS POVEY *bursts in up* RC. *She is a young person of about eighteen—rather formidable in appearance*)

DORIS (*moving down* R *of Lady Chesapeake*) Sorry to burst in like this, but I'm in terrible trouble . . .

LADY CHESAPEAKE. In trouble! (*To Price-Hargraves*) So this is your embarrassment? Don't bother to explain. You've said too much already, Mr Price-Hargraves.

DORIS. Actually, it's his secretary I want to see. Miss Spencer—she's my aunt. I was attacked by a man last night. It was dark.

PRICE-HARGRAVES (*looking at her*) It would have to be, wouldn't it!

DORIS. Well, I mean, it wasn't very nice. I mean, one doesn't expect that sort of thing to happen, does one?

PRICE-HARGRAVES. I certainly don't.

LADY CHESAPEAKE. Silence!

(BLOOM *enters up* RC)

BLOOME. I didn't mean to interrupt, but there was a . . .

LADY CHESAPEAKE. Go to your desk and be quiet.

(BLOOME *moves behind his desk*)

Go on, young woman.

DORIS. Well, last night I was just going home across Wandsworth Common when something moved behind a bush.

(*Bloome's telephone rings*)

LADY CHESAPEAKE. Mr Bloome, answer that. Tell them we're engaged.

BLOOME (*moving down* R *of the desk and lifting the receiver*) Lady Chesapeake and I are engaged!

LADY CHESAPEAKE. Really, Mr Bloome! (*To Doris*) Carry on.

(MISS SPENCER *enters up* RC *and moves between Doris and Lady Chesapeake*)

Doris. Auntie!
Miss Spencer. Doris! Poor Doris!
Price-Hargraves. Don't interrupt.

(Miss Spencer *moves up stage a little*)

What happened behind the bush?
Doris. I didn't wait to find out. I started to run, and this awful
thing chased me.
Lady Chesapeake. Well, I'm very sorry for you, but . . .
Doris. Sorry! How would you like to be chased across Wands-
worth Common?
Price-Hargraves. Yes, how would you like it, Lady Chesa-
peake?
Lady Chesapeake. Mr Price-Hargraves!
Doris. But he'll pay for it. Once the police find him . . .
Lady Chesapeake. Can you describe this man?
Doris. Of course I can. He was . . .
Lady Chesapeake. Just a minute. Mr Bloome, take this down.
Come along, come along, don't keep me waiting.

(Bloome *picks up a pad and pencil and stands behind Doris.* Doris
does not turn round to him)

Are you ready?
Bloome. Yes, Lady Chesapeake.
Lady Chesapeake (*to Doris*) Continue.
Doris. He was small and skinny.
Lady Chesapeake. Small and skinny.
Doris. With funny glasses.
Lady Chesapeake. Funny glasses.
Doris. And stringy hair.
Lady Chesapeake. Stringy hair. Is that all?
Doris. Oh, no. There's one thing I'd recognize anywhere. He
had a nervous cough.

(Bloome *coughs nervously.* Doris *stops abruptly, her movements
poised*)

I could have sworn . . .

(Bloome *coughs again*)

That cough! (*She turns to look at Bloome*) Skinny—stringy—that's him!
That's him! He's the one!

Doris *collapses against Lady Chesapeake, as—*

the Curtain *falls*

Scene 2

Scene—*the same. Nine o'clock the following morning.*

As the Curtain *rises, the factory hooter is sounding.* Price-Hargraves *and* Miss Spencer *are seated at their desks in grim silence. After a moment,* Price-Hargraves *looks at his watch, then at the empty desk down* R, *then at Miss Spencer.*

Price-Hargraves. Work, work, Miss Spencer! We must try to forget the terrible happenings of yesterday. (*He starts to look at a sheaf of papers, but realizes after a moment that he is holding them upside down*)

Miss Spencer (*suddenly, reading a letter*) Oh dear, oh my goodness —this is terrible! (*She rises and moves* R *of Price-Hargraves*) It must be their mistake. We couldn't possibly . . .

Price-Hargraves (*irritably*) Don't spither, Miss Drencer.

Miss Spencer. What!

Price-Hargraves. Can't you understand plain English? I said don't spither, Miss Drencer—I mean, don't drencer, Miss Smithers.

Miss Spencer. I'm not smithering.

Price-Hargraves. Please stop talking nonsense and tell me what has happened.

Miss Spencer. I'm sorry, Mr Price-Hargraves. It's from Meggitts of Hull. They say—oh dear . . .

Price-Hargraves. Is that *all* they say? Oh dear? "Dear Messrs Chunkibix—oh dear"?

Miss Spencer. It's their Christmas order. They ordered one hundred gross cartons of Chunkibix and we only sent one.

Price-Hargraves. Sent them one! But this is terrible! Let me see. (*He grabs the letter from Miss Spencer, and reads*) ". . . and we beg to inform one only sent." Somebody's head will roll for this! Whose head? Bloome's head. Bloome's dead! Bloome! (*He rises, goes to Bloome's desk, and takes an order book from the left-hand drawer*) Where's his order book? Let's see if I can find the right page. Here we are! One hundred gross cartons ordered and he only sent one. I've got him!

Miss Spencer. Yes, but . . . (*She points to the book*)

Price-Hargraves (*impressively*) "Remember", Miss Spencer. "Remember"—as poor Charles said before he lost his head.

Miss Spencer (*completely baffled*) Poor Charles—lost his head?

Price-Hargraves. You can't have taken history for your O-levels (*Patiently*) King Charles the First—lost his head on a scaffold in Whitehall.

Miss Spencer. But . . .

Price-Hargraves. Since when everyone else in Whitehall has been losing *theirs*.

Miss Spencer. But what's that to do with . . .

Price-Hargraves. I'm asking you to remember—remember—
remember!

Miss Spencer (*hopefully*) The fifth of November?

Price-Hargraves (*annoyed*) Tch—tch! Remember—"In the firm
of Chunkibix we do not tolerate moral looseness."

Miss Spencer. "Or careless work."

Price-Hargraves (*crossing below her and back to his desk*) "Or
avoidable errors"—(*largely*) "*Avoidable Errors!*"

Miss Spencer (*following to* c) Yes, but . . .

Price-Hargraves. This, on top of that shambles with the transistor radio . . .

Miss Spencer. But you don't understand . . .

Price-Hargraves. Of course I understand, Miss Spencer. When
Lady Chesapeake hears about this, Bloome will be "out!" Now sit
down, and let us relish the fact that soon we shall be "Bloomeless"!

(*They both sit at their desks*)

I don't suppose he'll have the nerve to show his face today.

(*There is a long pause as they silently peruse their papers. Then the
door up* RC *opens a crack, and a vague figure is seen.* Price-Hargraves
looks up. The door is gently closed. This is repeated twice. Eventually
Price-Hargraves *returns completely to his reading. The door opens
again, with agonizing slowness.* Bloome, *completely muffled in his raincoat,
with his hat on top, glides cringingly into the room. He starts to grope his
way to the hatstand, but* Price-Hargraves *looks up sharply.* Bloome
*flinches, goes straight to his desk, throws his coat nervously on the floor and
his bowler into the waste-paper basket, and sits at his desk. He gives his
nervous cough.* Price-Hargraves *and* Miss Spencer *watch him
relentlessly.* Bloome, *his hands shaking, starts to shuffle some papers and
ends by scattering them over the floor. He tries to open a drawer, but it
sticks. He hits the side of the desk and tries again. The drawer flies open,
scattering more papers, and* Bloome *falls on the floor. As he scrambles
back into his chair, there is a knock on the door up* RC)

Price-Hargraves. Come in!

(Harold *enters, carrying a ledger. He moves towards Price-Hargraves,
but never takes his eyes off Bloome. He offers it blindly to Price-Hargraves.*
Price-Hargraves, *his eyes also on Bloome, nearly falls off his chair as
he takes it*)

Thank you, Hopkins.

(Harold *moves back towards the door, still staring*)

(*Looking at the ledger*) Hopkins.

(Harold, *as before, returns*)

This is the wrong one. I asked for the "B" ledger. This is the "A".

Bloome (*suddenly jumping up*) Mr Price-Hargraves! I must speak!

This girl has made a terrible mistake—but you believe her. If I was guilty, do you think the police would allow me to walk up and down the street nilly-willy? Good heavens, no. They would be here to get me.

(*At this moment there is the wail of a siren, and a police car is heard to draw up outside*)

What's that?

PRICE-HARGRAVES. Well, it certainly isn't the ice-cream van!

(BLOOME *moves to the window behind his desk. His telephone rings. He tries to pick it up in a nonchalant way, imitating Price-Hargraves, but drops it on the floor*)

BLOOME (*shouting into the receiver*) Hello! Bloome here! . . . (*In a much quieter voice*) Oh. I'll come down. (*He replaces the receiver*) I think I'll just—go—down—stairs. (*Moving to the door up* RC) Nothing important—just the—er . . .

(BLOOME *exits up* RC, *miming a policeman as he goes*)

PRICE-HARGRAVES. Hopkins! The other ledger—as quick as you can.

(HAROLD *exits up* RC)

Oh, Miss Spencer—that it should come to this!

MISS SPENCER. You mean . . .

PRICE-HARGRAVES. The police within the precincts of Chunkibix. There hasn't been a sadder day since Sir Algernon caught his tie in the lift-gates. But I shall strive to move this scutch from our eblotcheon!

MISS SPENCER (*rising and moving* R *of him*) Oh, Mr Price-Hargraves, let us all scutch together! (*She places her hand on his*)

PRICE-HARGRAVES. What?

MISS SPENCER. Strive.

PRICE-HARGRAVES (*shrinking from her grip*) Yes, we shall together strive. What would I do without you? You are my right hand.

(MISS SPENCER *smiles*)

My standby.

(MISS SPENCER *smiles wider*)

My rock!

(MISS SPENCER *ceases to smile*)

(*Rising and heading for the door*) Miss Spencer, I'm going down to Invoices. Wait a minute, though! I mustn't leave you alone with that man—a man who is the subject of sudden lecherous impulses!

MISS SPENCER. Oh, Mr Price Hargraves!

PRICE-HARGRAVES (*returning to his desk*) I am sorry, Miss Spencer,

but we must call a shovel a bloody spade. Who can say when these
sex-storms may not break? That's what is so terrible about these
cases. You must not be the victim of such a storm.

Miss Spencer. I don't want to cause any inconvenience.

Price-Hargraves. Must we talk about conveniences, Miss
Spencer? I shall see that you are spared any embarrassment.

(*There is a knock at the door up* RC *and* Harold *enters with another
ledger*)

Out!

Harold. The "B" ledger.

Price-Hargraves (*angrily*) Put the B ledger on the desk and get
out. No—wait a minute. Sit down!

(Harold *sits* R *of Price-Hargraves' desk*)

(*Going and opening the door down* R) Miss Spencer, will you be good
enough to wait in here for a moment? I want to talk to Hopkins.
Rest assured I have your interest at heart.

Miss Spencer (*moving down* R) Oh, Mr Price-Hargraves!

(Miss Spencer *exits down* R *with a flourish.* Price-Hargraves,
*after a glance towards Harold, makes a great show of being "business-
like"*)

Price-Hargraves. Well, now—Hopkins.

Harold. Sir?

Price-Hargraves (*moving down* R *and bending over Bloome's waste-
paper basket as he places it farther below the desk*) Er—how long have
you been with us?

Harold (*involuntarily, but not loudly*) *Too* bloody long!

Price-Hargraves (*turning; startled*) *How* long did you say?

Harold (*meekly*) Two long years, sir.

Price-Hargraves. Oh! For a moment I thought you—(*he coughs*)
—two years.

Harold. Yes, sir.

Price-Hargraves (*again moving* R) *I* have been here *twenty-two*.

Harold (*again involuntarily but not loudly*) And don't you look it!

Price-Hargraves (*turning; sharply*) *What* did you say?

Harold. I said, sir, you don't look it, sir.

(Price-Hargraves *waggles a finger in one of his ears*)

Price-Hargraves (*moving pompously around*) Hopkins, what are
your duties here?

Harold (*with as much venom as he dare*) Running after you, mostly.

Price-Hargraves (*after a quick look at him*) Quite, quite. (*He
moves down* L; *smiling thinly*) "They also serve who only stand and
wait."

Harold (*muttering*) I don't get the chance to do much standing.

Price-Hargraves. Don't mutter, boy, don't mutter. (*He again*

waggles a finger in his ear) Hopkins, I am going to give you an oppor-
tunity to prove your worth. I am going to give you a task that . . .

HAROLD (*with a wail*) But I've got fifty letters (*gesturing*) out there,
sir, waiting to be stamped, and . . .

PRICE-HARGRAVES (*moving down* R; *gulping*) Hopkins—please!

HAROLD. But, I mean to say . . .

PRICE-HARGRAVES. Hopkins!

HAROLD (*muttering*) It isn't fair. Fifty letters waiting to . . .

PRICE-HARGRAVES. Speak up, boy! I can't hear a word you're
saying.

HAROLD (*under his breath; viciously*) Get a bloody ear trumpet.

(PRICE-HARGRAVES *now waggles fingers in both ears*)

PRICE-HARGRAVES (*not realizing he has his fingers in his ears still*)
What did you say? There's a buzzing in my ears.

HAROLD (*a little louder, but turning his head away*) Go and get
stuffed.

PRICE-HARGRAVES. What? (*He removes his fingers; irritably*) Bees-
wax!

HAROLD (*his voice throbbing with emotion*) I said: "Thank you very
much for the honour you are conferring on me, and I hope I shall
prove worthy of the confidence you are about to place in my cap-
abilities"! (*He takes a gasping breath*)

(PRICE-HARGRAVES *regards him very sceptically for a moment, then,
waggling his finger in his ear, moves to his desk, sits, and faces Harold*)

PRICE-HARGRAVES. Did you say all that the first time?

(HAROLD *nods*)

I must get my ears seen to. (*Impressively*) Hopkins, I hesitate to
mention this—er—deplorable subject to one so young and tender,
but—(*with a thin smile*)—"needs must when the devil drives", eh?

HAROLD (*agreeing*) Yeah, yeah, yeah.

PRICE-HARGRAVES (*after gulping hard*) You do know, I take it,
about—about Mr Bloome—and . . .

HAROLD (*very interested*) You mean about him chasing that dame
across Wandsworth Common the other night?

PRICE-HARGRAVES (*gulping again*) That is—er—more or less what I
mean.

HAROLD. 'Course I know. The whole building's talking about it,
sir. (*With a laugh*) Who'd have thought that Mr Bloome—at his
age . . .

PRICE-HARGRAVES. Hopkins!

HAROLD. Well, I mean to say! Why! He must be ; 3 old as *you!*

PRICE-HARGRAVES. *Hopkins!*

HAROLD (*oblivious*) Still—what is it they say, sir? "There's many
a good tune played on an old fiddle"! (*He gives Price-Hargraves a hefty
dig with his elbow*)

PRICE-HARGRAVES (*with a gulp; heavily*) I wonder if you *are* quite the person to undertake the task I had in mind!

HAROLD (*rising quickly*) P'raps not, sir! (*Moving speedily doorwards*) Shall I get back to them fifty letters?

PRICE-HARGRAVES (*fuming*) Sit down, boy!

(*Reluctantly*, HAROLD *sits again*)

(*After a slight pause*) Hopkins, this hitherto unsuspected—er—weakness of Mr Bloome's presents me with a problem.

HAROLD. Bet it presents *him* with one, too!

PRICE-HARGRAVES. *If* I might be allowed to continue——

HAROLD. You go right ahead, sir.

PRICE-HARGRAVES. —*without* interruptions! As I am perfectly sure you already know, charges have been made against Mr Bloome. Until such time as Mr Bloome is judged guilty (*offhandedly*) or, of course, otherwise, (*solemnly*) he will, I presume, continue with his duties here.

HAROLD. Got to admire his nerve, coming to work as if nothing had happened, haven't you, sir?

PRICE-HARGRAVES (*flatly*) Have you?

HAROLD (*with a look at him*) No, perhaps you *haven't.*

PRICE-HARGRAVES (*flatly*) I don't.

HAROLD. Come to think of it, I'm not to sure that I . . . (*He suddenly stops as a thought occurs to him*) Wow!

(PRICE-HARGRAVES *starts*)

And I'll tell you what! There's something we've got to bear in mind. Yes, sir!

PRICE-HARGRAVES (*frostily*) Indeed!

(*From now on*, HAROLD, *in his enthusiasm, forgets completely that he is talking to his "boss". He takes charge of the situation in no uncertain manner. He is not rude, merely carried away*)

HAROLD (*rising and pacing; very fervently*) I'll say. Mr Bloome chased that dame across Wandsworth Common the other night, didn't he, sir?

PRICE-HARGRAVES (*intensely disliking Harold's attitude*) Hopkins . . .

HAROLD (*holding up a silencing hand*) And we know what he was after, don't we?

PRICE-HARGRAVES (*with a yelp*) Hopkins, really, I . . .

HAROLD. Look, we're not kids, are we? We're men of the world, and we know that if he chased that dame across Wandsworth Common he wasn't just doing it to see who could get first to the other side! No, *sir!* He was after his . . .

PRICE-HARGRAVES (*in horror*) Hopkins!

HAROLD (*unheeding*) It's a kink he's got, see? A complex .'Cos you can bet your bottom dollar that the other night wasn't the first time, *and*—and this is what I'm getting at—you can take it from your Uncle Harold, it won't be the last!

PRICE-HARGRAVES (*in a defeated, pathetic bleat*) Hopkins!

HAROLD. I'm not blaming Mr Bloome, really. He can't help it! It's something that happens—suddenly—inside. (*He thumps his stomach with clenched fists*) He's as right as rain one minute, and then —wham! He sees a woman—something gets him, and . . . (*He faces Price-Hargraves, crouches down a little and gives a long, low, sexy growl*) Urrrrrr!

(PRICE-HARGRAVES, *battered and beaten, almost slides out of his chair, his eyes popping*)

(*Sweeping on*) And, you see, trouble is, he never knows when it's going to happen. And—(*stabbing the desk with one finger*)—what's more to the point, neither do we! Believe you me, it's just as likely to happen to him here, *in this office*, as anywhere else.

PRICE-HARGRAVES (*attempting to assert himself*) Hopkins, that is precisely what I . . .

HAROLD (*irritably waving a hand for silence*) Just as likely! When the sex-bug gets you, you don't worry about moonlight nights and sylvan glades and all that hooey. You've got to do something about it, even if you're in an office smothered in Order Forms.

(PRICE-HARGRAVES *ineffectually and slowly slaps the top of his desk*)

So, I tell you, *we've* got to do something—otherwise there won't be a dame in this office who'll be safe. (*Looking towards the door* R) And when I think . . . ! (*In horror*) Gawd! If he tried his tricks on her! Ooooh! (*The thought is so appalling that it takes the wind out of his sails. He totters to his chair and collapses on it*)

PRICE-HARGRAVES (*seizing the chance to take charge*) Precisely. (*He rises, somewhat unsteadily, and moves* R *of Harold*) And it was with that very—er—contingency in mind—one which, I must say, for one so young, you have grasped with—er—disturbing alacrity . . .

HAROLD. I can't get it out of my mind! If anything happened to *her*—I don't know what I'd do!

(HAROLD *is, of course, thinking of Fiona.* PRICE-HARGRAVES *is not*)

PRICE-HARGRAVES. I would cut off Bloome's right hand.

HAROLD. Eh? (*Irritably*) It isn't his *hand* you want to worry about.

PRICE-HARGRAVES. H'm! (*With vigour*) Hopkins, the strong must defend the weak!

(HAROLD *looks puzzled*)

(*Acidly*) You and I, Hopkins.

HAROLD (*vaguely*) Oh, yeah, yeah.

PRICE-HARGRAVES. Just so long as that—that bedevilled maniac —just so long as Mr Bloome is at large. And that will only be until Lady Chesapeake hears about the orders he's mucked up. Just so

long, Hopkins, you and I must be on the alert for any sign of—
er . . .

HAROLD. Hanky-panky.

PRICE-HARGRAVES. Hanky—Hopkins, I would be grateful if you
would allow me to say what I have to say without interruption.
From this moment forth, Hopkins, our first duty is the protection of
the weaker sex. All else must take second place.

HAROLD (*blinking*) Even those fifty letters waiting to be sealed
and . . .

PRICE-HARGRAVES. Damn the letters!

HAROLD (*cheerfully*) Yes, *sir!*

PRICE-HARGRAVES. Now, as you know, Hopkins, I am constantly
having to leave the office . . .

HAROLD. Yes, sir. I know. My poor dad's the same.

PRICE-HARGRAVES. What?

HAROLD. Doctor says it's his age—and there's nothing you can
do about it.

PRICE-HARGRAVES (*firmly*) Hopkins, on the numerous occasions
when my presence is required in other departments, it will be your
duty to police this office. Never, not for one single moment, must
Mr Bloome be left in here alone with that poor dear, defenceless
creature.

HAROLD. In . . . ? But she isn't in here, sir. (*Indicating the door
down* R) That's where she works.

PRICE-HARGRAVES (*explosively*) What the . . . ? Who the devil are
you talking about?

HAROLD. Why—Fiona!

PRICE-HARGRAVES (*lost*) Fiona?

HAROLD. Miss Jones. Isn't that who you . . . ?

PRICE-HARGRAVES. Hopkins, I am referring to Miss Spencer!

HAROLD. Miss . . . ? (*Reprovingly*) Oh, no, sir! Oh, no! Be fair!
I don't think Mr Bloome is *that* far gone!

PRICE-HARGRAVES. Hopkins!

(*There is a piercing scream off down* R)

HAROLD (*rising*) My gawd! He's started! Fiona!

(HAROLD and PRICE-HARGRAVES *move to the door down* R. MISS
SPENCER *rushes in, followed by* FIONA, *runs across to the desk* LC *and
screams.* MISS SPENCER *jumps up on the chair* R *of the desk,* FIONA *sits on
the edge of the desk*)

PRICE-HARGRAVES. Miss Spencer! (*To Hopkins*) In you go! Deal
with him as you think fit.

HAROLD. Yes, sir!

(HAROLD *exits* R)

FIONA. It's all right, Miss Spencer. It's all over now. It's all over.

PRICE-HARGRAVES. All over! (*Astonished*) That was a quick job, wasn't it?

FIONA. Miss Spencer has had a shock, sir.

MISS SPENCER. Dreadful, dreadful!

FIONA. A mouse, wasn't it, Miss Spencer? Jumped out of the waste-paper basket and ran right up Miss Spencer's . . . She got such a shock!

PRICE-HARGRAVES. Miss Jones!

FIONA. It came down again, sir!

PRICE-HARGRAVES. Perhaps *it* got a shock, too.

(HAROLD *dashes in down* R)

HAROLD. Where is he? I'll kill him! I'll break him in two, I'll tear him limb from limb. Where is he?

(BLOOME *enters up* RC *and moves behind Harold*)

BLOOME. Who are you looking for?

(HAROLD *screams and jumps into Price-Hargraves' arms.* PRICE-HARGRAVES *drops him.* HAROLD, FIONA *and* MISS SPENCER *crouch* L *of Price-Hargraves for protection*)

(R *of Price-Hargraves*) Sorry I've been so long. I was downstairs in the office. In an identification parade. The policeman said to that girl: "Would you mind pointing out the man who jumped out at you," and she pointed straight at me! (*Plaintively*) Shouldn't there have been more than me in the line-up?

PRICE-HARGRAVES. Bloome, I can stand no more! I'm going down to Invoices.

BLOOME (*shaking Price-Hargraves by the hand*) Good-bye, sir. (*He moves behind his desk*)

PRICE-HARGRAVES. I'm coming back! Miss Jones, go to your office. Leave your door open.

FIONA. But I'll be in a draught.

PRICE-HARGRAVES. You'll be in much more than that if you don't. Don't forget, Hopkins.

(PRICE-HARGRAVES *exits up* RC. FIONA *exits down* R. MISS SPENCER *sits at her desk. There is a pause.* HAROLD *does a policeman's knees-bend*)

BLOOME. Everything all right, Hopkins?

HAROLD (*with another bend*) Well, I . . .

BLOOME. Miss Spencer and I can deal with whatever we have to do, without your help. (*He shuts the door Fiona has left open, and propels Harold towards the door up* RC)

HAROLD (*trying to continue bending*) Er—yes, sir, but Mr Price . . .

BLOOME. I wish to be alone with Miss Spencer. Out.

(BLOOME *pushes* HAROLD *out up* RC. MISS SPENCER *flutters the pages of her shorthand notebook frantically*)

Lost your place, Miss Spencer?

Miss Spencer. No—no, I know my place . . .

Bloome (*taking a letter from his desk*) Miss Spencer, I'm going to . . . (*He moves towards her*)

Miss Spencer (*leaping up and diving behind the window curtains behind her*) No! No! You're not!

(Lady Chesapeake *enters up* RC)

Lady Chesapeake. Mr Price- . . . Miss Spencer! What is going on here?

(Bloome *returns to his desk hastily*)

Where's Mr Price-Hargraves? *Where is* Mr Price-Hargraves?

Miss Spencer (*peeping round the curtain*) He's gone down to Invoices.

Lady Chesapeake. Leaving you alone with—has the man no sense? You will go to my room. I will find you something to do there. At once.

(Miss Spencer *scurries out up* RC)

(*To Bloome*) Tell Mr Price-Hargraves I will see him in my office after lunch. One more thing, Mr Bloome, the name for our new cocktail biscuits . . .

Bloome. You mean "Red Hot Chasers"?

Lady Chesapeake. Alter it! One red hot chaser in the firm is enough.

(Lady Chesapeake *exits up* RC)

Bloome (*moving* C) Innocent! I'm innocent! I've never done anything like that! Innocent! I'm going to end it all. (*He climbs on the chair* R *of the desk, holds the end of his tie in the air, and jumps off*) Oh, blow it! (*He gets on the chair again*)

(Price-Hargraves *enters up* RC)

Price-Hargraves. Bloome, if you want to hang up your suit, get out of it first. What are you doing up there?

Bloome (*getting down*) Getting down.

Price-Hargraves. I want to know what is going on. Has this girl actually preferred charges?

Bloome. Yes.

Price-Hargraves. So you will have to appear in court.

Bloome. Yes.

Price-Hargraves. Have you got a solicitor?

Bloome. Yes, I had to have one when I bought my bungalow.

Price-Hargraves. What's their name?

Bloome. Hunter and Dewar.

Price-Hargraves. Hunter and . . . (*Horrified*) Good heavens, man, you can't use a firm with names like that!

Bloome. No?

PRICE-HARGRAVES. You must get another solicitor.

BLOOME. Why, are they any good?

PRICE-HARGRAVES. Not in the least, but you have to have them.

BLOOME. I see.

PRICE-HARGRAVES (*moving above the end of Bloome's desk*) That detective who was here—what did he come for?

BLOOME. Gum.

PRICE-HARGRAVES. What?

BLOOME. Gum. That's his name. Gum.

PRICE-HARGRAVES (*fuming*) Gum! You'll come to a sticky end. What did he want? What did he say?

BLOOME (*moving up* c) Well, he said that that girl—what's *her* name?

PRICE-HARGRAVES (*still fuming*) Damn her name! What about her?

BLOOME (*moving to the hatstand*) She has no doubts whatever that it was me who—you know—Gum says, and Gum says she'll swear to it in Court. That's what Gum says.

PRICE-HARGRAVES. What else does Gum say?

BLOOME. Gum says she'll be given every chance of ruining me. Gum says. (*He leans against the hatstand*)

PRICE-HARGRAVES. After all, it would be her turn to try.

(BLOOME *gasps*)

(*Moving towards Bloome; menacingly*) Bloome! Do you know what you are up against?

BLOOME (*shrinking*) Yes, the hatstand.

PRICE-HARGRAVES (*sitting at his desk*) I shall write to my solicitor and ask him to defend you. He's a good chap—once got me out of a bloody mess . . . (*He breaks off hurriedly*) Looks after all my legal affairs. Now, let me see. (*Suddenly*) Where's Miss Spencer? (*Rising and advancing on Bloome*) Bloome! You haven't . . . ?

BLOOME. No, I haven't. I didn't get the chance.

PRICE-HARGRAVES. What!

BLOOME (*moving down* RC) Lady Chesapeake took her along to the office.

PRICE-HARGRAVES (*astonished*) Lady Chesapeake took her . . . ?

BLOOME. She thought Miss Spencer would be safer there than here.

PRICE-HARGRAVES. Safer than here? Oh, the ignominy—the shame! It's fearful! But fearful things have to be faced. (*Moving to Bloome*) Even you, Bloome, have to be faced. (*Taking his arm and leading him down* c) Now, when you see my solicitor, you will tell him that the charge is utterly untrue. That the girl's made a mistake. Then——

BLOOME. But I've already . . .

PRICE-HARGRAVES (*sweeping him aside*) —that on the night in question you were nowhere near Wandsworth Common——

(BLOOME *opens his mouth to speak*)

(*Silencing him*)—that never in your life have you been on Wandsworth Common——

BLOOME. But, Mr Price- ...

PRICE-HARGRAVES (*with an enormous silencing gesture*) —that until this charge was brought against you, you had scarcely even *heard* of Wandsworth Common! *And*, on that night, far from being on Wandsworth Common, you were miles away in your home at—at— (*Snapping*) where *do* you live, by the way?

BLOOME. Wandsworth Common.

CURTAIN

ACT II

SCENE I

SCENE—*The same. About midnight, the following evening.*
The office is decorated with balloons, streamers and other Christmas decorations and looks quite festive.

When the CURTAIN *rises,* BLOOME *is seated at his desk blowing up a balloon. He is in evening dress and wears an incongruous "funny hat". Several deflated balloons lie on his desk and one, with a grinning face painted on it, is attached to a string which is held down by a paper-weight, and floats a couple of feet in the air. Music and chatter can be heard off up* R. BLOOME *blows and blows. When the balloon is almost filled, there is a knock at the door.*

BLOOME. Come in!

(*The balloon immediately deflates as* BLOOME *removes his mouth from it to speak. He is very annoyed.* HAROLD, *also in evening dress with paper hat, enters*)

HAROLD. Ah!

BLOOME (*trying to stop the balloon going down*) Grrr!

HAROLD. Havin' fun?

BLOOME. What d'you want?

HAROLD. Mr Price-Hargraves' compliments to Mr Bloome, and has he finished blowing up the balloons yet?

BLOOME. Mr Bloome's compliments to Mr Price-Hargraves and he hasn't.

HAROLD. Well, Mr Price-Hargraves' compliments to Mr Bloome and will he get a move on, 'cos they'll be wantin' 'em soon for the balloon dance.

BLOOME (*angrily*) Mr Bloome's compliments to Mr Price-Hargraves and if he wants the balloons he can—can . . .

HAROLD (*excitedly*) Go on—go on!

BLOOME (*limply*) Have 'em in ten minutes. (*He begins to blow up another one*)

HAROLD. Ten minutes?

BLOOME (*removing the balloon, which promptly goes down*) Ten hours. You wouldn't like to give me a hand, would you, Hopkins?

HAROLD (*pleasantly*) No.

BLOOME. No. (*Looking at him*) Does your *mother* like you?

HAROLD (*ignoring this*) Coo! Ain't half a party downstairs. Smashin'! You don't know what you're missing. Er—but you're not going to have the nerve to show *your* face at it, are you.

BLOOME. Well, if you've had the nerve to show yours, I don't see . . .

HAROLD. You don't want all the women to run screaming home, do you?

BLOOME. Are you suggesting that my face . . .

HAROLD. Once you arrive at the party and the women see that hungry look in your eyes . . .

BLOOME. But I'm not hungry.

HAROLD. Not for fish-paste, p'raps not! But we know the kind of night starvation you suffer from, don't we?

BLOOME. Do we?

(HAROLD *gives a long, low sexy growl*)

I beg your pardon?

(HAROLD *repeats the growl*)

Hopkins, I trust that was only your stomach rumbling!

(*Bloome's telephone rings.* HAROLD *answers it*)

HAROLD. Oh hell—hello? Hopkins here . . . Yes, Mr Collinson . . . Whisky? Only eleven bottles? (*He looks enquiringly at Bloome*)

BLOOME. What?

HAROLD. Mr Collinson from the dance floor—says there were only eleven bottles in the last batch of whisky you sent down.

BLOOME. But I sent twelve.

HAROLD (*on the phone*) His Royal Sexiness says . . .

(BLOOME *looks horriffied*)

I mean, Mr Bloome says he sent twelve . . . Eh? (*To Bloome*) Only eleven arrived. (*He rings off*)

BLOOME. Well, go and see about it. (*To himself*) Royal Sss . . . ! (*Imitating Price-Hargraves, but with a shaking hand*) Out! (*He steadies the shaking hand with his other one*)

(HAROLD *begins to dart out, then pulls himself up and returns to Bloome's desk*)

HAROLD. Hey, who do you think you are?

(PRICE-HARGRAVES, *also wearing an incongruous paper hat, appears in the doorway up* RC. BLOOME *does not see him*)

BLOOME. Bloome-Hargraves. I mean—(*repeating the gesture*)—out!

PRICE-HARGRAVES. Mr Bloome!

BLOOME (*pointing without looking*) Out!

PRICE-HARGRAVES. *Bloome!*

BLOOME (*seeing him; with a yelp*) *In!* (*Rising*) Do come in, Mr Price-Hargraves! Hopkins, a chair for Mr Price-Hargraves.

PRICE-HARGRAVES (*fuming*) Mr Bloome, can you tell me one thing?

BLOOME. Several, Mr Price-Hargraves, several.
PRICE-HARGRAVES (*thundering*) Who the hell do you think you are?
HAROLD. He's got an idea he's you, Mr Price-Hargraves.
PRICE-HARGRAVES. Has he, indeed!
HAROLD. But he isn't, is he? I mean, he hasn't got your stomach
to begin with, and . . .
PRICE-HARGRAVES. *Out!*

(HAROLD "*outs*" *rapidly up* RC)

Bloome!
BLOOME. Yes, Mr Price-Hargraves? I'm sorry if I . . .
PRICE-HARGRAVES. Balloons. (*He moves away*)
BLOOME (*muttering*) Balloons to you. (*He begins to blow up a balloon*)

PRICE-HARGRAVES (*turning*) *What* did you say?

(BLOOME, *blowing, makes an incomprehensible reply*)

Bloome, are you aware that the balloon dance begins in about
twenty minutes?

(BLOOME, *blowing, nods his head violently*)

And that sixty inflated balloons are required?

(BLOOME *nods again*)

And how many are inflated already? (*Pointing to it*) One, Bloome,
one! One miserable one!

(BLOOME, *with balloon in mouth, makes a gesture of holding up two
fingers*)

(*Mistaking Bloome's meaning*) Bloome!

(BLOOME *repeats the gesture twice*)

Bloome, how dare you! If Lady Chesapeake . . .

(BLOOME *frantically repeats the gesture three times*)

Bloome, this is too much! To suggest that I should—er—(*repeating
Bloome's gesture*) is bad enough! But to intimate that Lady Chesa-
peake can do the same! It—it borders on blasphemy.
BLOOME (*finishing the balloon and removing it from his mouth*) Two.
PRICE-HARGRAVES. What?
BLOOME. Two balloons blown up. (*He holds up two fingers*) You said
only one.
PRICE-HARGRAVES (*leaning over Bloome's desk*) Bloome!
BLOOME (*holding up his fingers again*) Two!
PRICE-HARGRAVES (*fuming*) I—I . . .
BLOOME (*starting to laugh*) And you thought I meant . . .(*He holds
up his fingers again*)
PRICE-HARGRAVES (*slapping at the fingers*) Stop doing that!

Bloome (*roaring with laughter*) I meant—(*he holds up his fingers*)—
and you thought I meant—(*he holds up his fingers again, laughing*)

Price-Hargraves. *Bloome!*

Bloome. You—(*holding up his fingers*)—and Lady Chesapeake—
(*holding up his fingers*) Ooo! You've got a nasty mind.

(Price-Hargraves *snatches the balloon from Bloome's other hand.
It immediately deflates.* Price-Hargraves *rages as he tries to stop it*)

(*Holding up one finger*) One!

Price-Hargraves. Bloome, sixty inflated balloons are required
in twenty minutes. Sixty, Bloome! You will inflate them—or else!
One balloon every twenty seconds, Bloome—or else!

Bloome. I'll do my best.

Price-Hargraves. Your best? Is that all? You'll have to do a
great deal better than that.

Bloome. I don't seem to have the breath.

Price-Hargraves. Perhaps you're saving it for your next chase
across Wandsworth Common.

Bloome. Oh, Mr Price-Hargraves, that was below the belt.

Price-Hargraves (*significantly*) No doubt. (*He takes a balloon
from the desk and hands it grandly to Bloome*) Blow, Bloome, blow!

Bloome. But . . .

Price-Hargraves. Twenty seconds have gone, Bloome—one
balloon behind.

(Bloome *blows a balloon frantically, having difficulties*)

Blow, Bloome, blow!

Bloome (*removing the balloon*) I am. (*He yelps as it starts to deflate
and quickly puts it in his mouth again*)

Price-Hargraves (*his cheeks blowing out as he instructs Bloome*)
Blow, blow, thou blooming Bloome!

(Bloome *gives a violent blow. The balloon shoots out of his mouth
and whirls around deflating. They try to catch it.* Bloome *staggers to his
desk and sits*)

Bloome. It's no use, Mr Price-Hargraves. There isn't a blooming
blow left in me.

Price-Hargraves (*exasperatedly*) Good heavens, man, it's simple.
All you have to do is . . . (*He picks up a balloon—specially prepared with
pin-pricks so that it will not inflate*) Watch! (*He blows—no result. He looks
embarrassedly at Bloome*)

Bloome (*politely*) I'm watching.

Price-Hargraves. All you have to do is . . . (*He breathes in noisily,
expanding his chest, then blows. No result*)

Bloome. Ah! I see now. Thank you, Mr Price-Hargraves. (*He
breathes in deeply, quickly inflates a balloon, fastens it with a paper-clip,
picks up another and does the same*)

(*Meanwhile* PRICE-HARGRAVES *is staggering* LC, *tying himself in knots as he tries to inflate his balloon*)

PRICE-HARGRAVES (*gasping*) All you have to do is . . .
BLOOME (*triumphantly*) Mr Price-Hargraves! Look at mine! (*He holds up a balloon in each hand*)

(PRICE-HARGRAVES, *raging, returns to his blowing, clinging to his desk and kneeling on the floor*)

Blow, Mr Price-Hargraves, blow. Blow—thou winter wind!
PRICE-HARGRAVES. It's so simple . . . (*He lies on his back on the floor*)
BLOOME. Twenty seconds gone!
PRICE-HARGRAVES (*gasping*) Child's play! (*He gives a hollow groan, closes his eyes and, gasping for breath, lies with arms outstretched*)

(BLOOME *rushes across to him and inserts a blown-up balloon into Price-Hargraves' mouth*)

BLOOME (*standing back*) Well done, Mr Price-Hargraves, well done! My goodness, what a blow.

(PRICE-HARGRAVES *sits up, the balloon still in his mouth, and gapes at it*)

Now I'll fetch you a few more, and . . . (*He goes to his desk*)

(PRICE-HARGRAVES *leaps up in a fury, still gasping, and grabs his paper-knife. He stabs the balloon viciously and bursts it*)

Mr Price-Hargraves!

(PRICE-HARGRAVES *staggers across to Bloome's desk and stabs each blown-up balloon in turn, bursting it*)

Mr Price-Hargraves—the balloon dance!
PRICE-HARGRAVES (*picking up the last balloon*) The balloon dance——
BLOOME. Yes, yes, the balloon dance, in twenty minutes!
PRICE-HARGRAVES (*loudly, gasping*) —the balloon dance—will be replaced by—the Gay Gordons! (*He staggers* C *and sits* R *of his desk*)
BLOOME. But will Lady Chesapeake . . .
PRICE-HARGRAVES (*still gasping*) Lady Chesapeake can—(*he automatically lifts two fingers, then, realizing what he has done, groans and covers the guilty hand with the other one*)
BLOOME. Right. I'll go and tell her. (*He moves to the door*)
PRICE-HARGRAVES (*roaring*) You will not!
BLOOME. I mean—about the Gay Gordons.
PRICE-HARGRAVES. I'll tell her myself—when I have recovered my equilibrium.
BLOOME (*looking round*) Where did you put it?
PRICE-HARGRAVES (*with a gasping sigh*) I'm not as young as I was, Bloome.

BLOOME. Oh, don't say that!

PRICE-HARGRAVES. It's true—true! (*Putting his hand on his stomach*) And I can't mix my drinks as I used to. (*He is struck by a sudden thought and a look of low cunning comes over his face*) Yes—go and tell her!

BLOOME. What?

PRICE-HARGRAVES. Lady Chesapeake—go and tell her.

BLOOME. But you said . . .

PRICE-HARGRAVES (*rising*) Well, go and tell somebody something.

BLOOME. What are you talking . . .

PRICE-HARGRAVES (*pushing Bloome up* RC) Blow up more balloons, blow up Lady Chesapeake, blow up the record-player—*out!*

(PRICE-HARGRAVES *pushes* BLOOME *off up* RC, *then goes quickly below his own desk, opens a panel in the downstage side and reveals a bottle of whisky and a glass. He pours a drink and knocks it back. As he does so,* BLOOME *opens the door a crack, peeps in, sees what is happening, and nips down behind his own desk.* PRICE-HARGRAVES *cunningly marks the liquid level with a pencil, replaces bottle and glass, and tiptoes out up* RC *with a satisfied grin.* BLOOME *immediately emerges, goes to the desk, cannot open it, and bangs it as he did his own desk in the previous scene. The panel flies open. He takes out the glass and bottle, picks up a rubber and starts to erase the mark.* PRICE-HARGRAVES *bursts in down* R)

PRICE-HARGRAVES. Haa!

(BLOOME *starts convulsively and tries to hide the bottle*)

The missing bottle! So you pinch bottles as well as bottoms! Bloome —is there no limit to your perfidy?

(BLOOME *gapes and waggles the bottle at him*)

(*Quickly*) Oh well, now you've done it we might as well share it. Get yourself a glass. (*He snatches the bottle and his own glass and starts to pour*)

BLOOME. Well—just a small one. (*He goes to his own desk and returns with a pint tumbler*)

(PRICE-HARGRAVES *stares at the pint glass, then, having filled his own, starts to fill this as well, with helping nudges from* BLOOME. *He then juggles the glasses so that* BLOOME *gets the small one and he himself is left with the large*)

PRICE-HARGRAVES. To Lady Chesapeake, and all who sail in her!

(*They drink,* BLOOME *finishing his quickly and gazing at* PRICE-HARGRAVES *as he slowly drains the big tumbler.* PRICE-HARGRAVES *replaces bottle and both glasses and closes the panel*)

BLOOME (*moving to the desk and picking up a paper trumpet*) Well, come on, let's go to the dance.

PRICE-HARGRAVES. You're not going to any dance! There are decent ladies down there. Common-chasing absolutely verboten! You are going to do the accounts.

(PRICE-HARGRAVES *pushes Bloome to his desk, snatches the trumpet, taps Bloome over the head with it, and exits up* RC *with a swagger—and a slight stagger.* BLOOME *sits at his desk and picks up a small adding machine, which he starts to work, muttering*)

BLOOME. I'll get these done and go down. He'll be too stoned to notice!

(FIONA *enters up* RC *wearing a paper hat and a very sexy party dress. She discards the hat on Bloome's desk and slinks up to him*)

FIONA. Lovely party, isn't it, Mr Bloome?
BLOOME. Is it? I don't know—I haven't been allowed—I haven't been down yet. Do you want something?

(FIONA *ogles him*)

From this room, I mean?
FIONA (*leaning all over him across the desk*) I just came up to rest for a bit.
BLOOME (*indicating the desk* LC) Well, sit over there. There's more room. (*He works the adding machine frantically*)

(FIONA *pouts, but moves to sit on the desk* LC)

FIONA (*taking off her shoes*) These shoes are killing me. (*She puts them in the "In" tray*)
BLOOME. Miss Jones, do you mind if I make a suggestion?
FIONA. Ooooh, Mr Bloome!
BLOOME (*rising and moving* R *of her*) Would you mind not putting your shoes in Mr Price-Hargraves' "In" tray? If he comes *in* you'll be *out*, and I'll be *pending*! (*He reaches for the shoes*)
FIONA (*grabbing his hand and pulling him down* C) Don't speak! Don't say anything for a moment! I can feel it going right down my spine.
BLOOME (*drawing her away* LC) Well, don't stand under it. I know what you're here for.
FIONA. Yes, Mr Bloome?
BLOOME. I'll go and get your boy-friend. (*He moves to the door up* RC) Harold!
FIONA (*running after him*) No! (*She slams the door and starts pushing him* C *until he is wedged against the desk* LC) You see, he's a nice lad, Harold. But he's young and inexperienced. There's so much he's got to learn. I'm sure there's a lot you could teach him. (*She pushes herself close against his chest*)
BLOOME. Please—Miss Jones—Hopkins!
FIONA (*nestling and fondling him*) 'Course there are some things you can't learn. I mean—you either have them or you haven't.
BLOOME. Oh?
FIONA. And you have them!
BLOOME. Have I? Where? I don't remember bringing them.
FIONA. They're all saying so.

BLOOME. All?

FIONA. Every female in the place. Miss Fenton said just now . . .

BLOOME. Miss Fenton?

FIONA. Miss Fenton. Invoices. She said she thought the men in this building were the dullest, mouldiest bunch of squares in London——

BLOOME (*moving away* LC) *Did* she . . .

FIONA. —except you, she said. (*Vamping him again*) She said you only have to look into your eyes and it's all there.

BLOOME. Whose eyes?

FIONA. Yours, Mr Bloome. (*She suddenly grabs him*)

BLOOME (*struggling free*) Hey! Hey! Miss Jones—the door, the door! (*He runs up* RC)

FIONA (*chasing after him*) Miss Potter said she'd seen it too!

BLOOME (*opening the door*) I don't remember showing Miss Potter . . .

FIONA (*slamming the door and dragging him back to the desk* LC) She said she'd seen the hungry fire deep down inside! The fire that drove you out into the darkness of the night searching for someone to put it out. Mr Bloome—warm me with that fire! (*She lies back across the desk and pulls Bloome over her*)

(MISS SPENCER *enters up* RC, *wearing a fez*)

MISS SPENCER. Mr Bloome! Miss Jones! I'm sorry—I didn't know . . .

BLOOME (*scrambling from under Fiona*) Here comes the fire chief! (*He moves to his own desk, tidying himself*)

MISS SPENCER. I came in for an aspirin. (*She goes to her own desk, looking very embarrassed*)

BLOOME. We—er—we were just adjusting Mr Price-Hargraves' desk calender—it—er—sticks . . .

MISS SPENCER. H'm . . .

BLOOME. Have you a headache?

MISS SPENCER. It's nothing. I'm afraid I rather over-indulged. Too much fizzy lemonade. Are you enjoying yourself, Mr Bloome?

BLOOME. Yes, thank you—(*referring to Miss Spencer's fez*)—Mrs Cooper.

MISS SPENCER (*removing the fez*) Are *you* enjoying yourself, Miss Jones?

FIONA (*snatching her shoes*) I was—until you came in!

(FIONA *exits up* RC *angrily.* BLOOME *starts after her, but* MISS SPENCER *moves smartly to close the door*)

MISS SPENCER. Really—young girls today.

BLOOME (*moving to the filing cabinet and fiddling with the pencil sharpener*) Oh, they mean well. (*He absent-mindedly sticks his finger in the sharpener and turns the handle, then shrieks*)

MISS SPENCER. They're so impertinent—so self-willed.

BLOOME (*nursing his finger*) So pointed. (*Moving to the door*) Miss Spencer, I'll leave you.

MISS SPENCER (*flinging him from the door into his desk chair*) Oh, but I can't drive you out. You said you were going to work.

BLOOME. That can wait. (*He starts to rise*)

MISS SPENCER (*pushing him back*) It seems so unfair. I mean, you were here first.

BLOOME. Miss Spencer, I don't want to embarrass you—me being here—you having to talk to me—I'll leave you . . . (*He tries to rise again*)

MISS SPENCER. No. (*She flings him back*) You shan't go. Why should you?

BLOOME. Because I know my presence must offend you.

MISS SPENCER (*fiercely*) Why should it? Why should it offend me and not Miss Jones? I don't suppose you gave a moment's thought to the possibility that your presence might offend her, did you? And yet with me it's the first thing that springs to your mind. Why should it?

BLOOME. Well—you're different from Miss Jones. (*He vaguely contrasts the two shapes with his hands*)

MISS SPENCER (*moving away c and not noticing this*) You mean I'm older.

BLOOME (*rising and moving R of her*) No—well, yes. But it's not that. Miss Jones is not so sensitive.

MISS SPENCER (*excitedly*) Why don't you say what you mean, Mr Bloome? Why don't you say "because Miss Jones is not so narrow-minded"? That's what you think, isn't it? You think it, everyone thinks it—and I know it! I know it!

BLOOME. You mustn't upset yourself. I'm sorry . . .

MISS SPENCER (*stamping on his toe*) *Stop* being sorry! What have you got to be sorry about?

BLOOME (*hopping about on one foot*) I'm sorry for you . . .

MISS SPENCER. Pity. That's all I've ever had all my life. Pity!

BLOOME. What does it matter? You have your pride. (*Melodramatically*) You have your pride and you can be proud of yourself, Miss Spencer, because in the face of all temptation you have been true to yourself. This above all—to thine own self be true. (*Declaiming*) Then it must follow as the night the day, thou can'st not then be false to any man. Whether it is nobler in the mind to bear the slings and arrows of something fortune—or whether it is better to bury Caesar . . .

MISS SPENCER. Oh, shut up!

BLOOME. I beg your pardon?

MISS SPENCER. All that rot about being true to myself in the face of all temptation! What temptation? Nobody's ever tempted me in my life . . .

BLOOME. Well, that's good . . .

MISS SPENCER. And as far as I can see, nobody ever will!

BLOOME. Oh, I don't know . . .

MISS SPENCER (*moving above the desk* LC *and storming on*) I shall go to my grave knowing as much about life as I did when I was a child. When I was young and asked questions about—well, you know—all I got in reply was a mumbling about the birds and the bees. Always the birds and the—bloody bees! I'm not a bird! I'm not a bee! I didn't know what they were talking about then, and to all practical purposes I still don't. I shall go on living my drab lonely life—ridiculed and despised by everyone—the girls in the office—the men . . .

BLOOME. Not everybody—not Mr Price-Hargraves . . .

MISS SPENCER. That old goat!

(BLOOME *gasps*)

(*Starting to throw things about*) I'm going out of my mind. (*She picks up papers, books, pads, trays, the pot of flowers, a bowl of paper-clips from the desk and throws them all over the room*) Please somebody—anybody—take me home! (*She moves* L *of the desk, hurling books and directories to the floor from the table* L) I want to go home—I want to go home—ooooooh! (*She moves below the desk as she reaches a climax, grabs the telephone, and is about to throw it across the room*)

(BLOOME *seizes the telephone just in time, replaces it quickly, and slaps her face. She stops yelling instantly and stares at him*)

BLOOME (*backing away in horror*) Oh, I'm sorry. I didn't mean to do that.

MISS SPENCER (*enraptured*) You brute! You magnificent brute!

BLOOME. Yes, well—(*he kneels on the floor and starts picking things up*)

MISS SPENCER. You struck me! You struck *me!* On the films I've seen it done so often. In books I've read about it times out of count. And always I've hoped—I've prayed—that one day someone would —*and you have!*

BLOOME. Miss Spencer, I can assure you it hurt me more than it hurt . . .

MISS SPENCER. Don't say that! (*Gazing in front of her*) Don't take this moment away from me. I want to feel that stinging blow burning my cheek for the rest of my life. (*Standing very close to his kneeling figure*) I want to carry for ever in my mind's eye the picture of you— *towering* above me in all your manly compelling strength.

BLOOME. My knees were knocking . . .

MISS SPENCER (*kneeling beside him*) Your eyes were like twin burning coals of fire!

BLOOME. They're smokeless fuel! (*He runs away from her on his knees, to* L *of his own desk*)

MISS SPENCER (*pursuing him on her knees*) My eyes are opened at last. You have opened them! (*She pins him against the desk*)

BLOOME. Well, shut them . . .

Miss Spencer. I see now what my life has lacked—a master! (*She grabs Bloome*)

(Price-Hargraves *enters up* RC)

Price-Hargraves (*hurrying down* C) Miss Spencer! Don't tell me Bloome has . . .

Bloome (*scrambling up against the desk*) I have not!

Price-Hargraves. What have you done to Miss Spencer?

Bloome. I had to hit her, to stop her bawling. (*He climbs through the knee-hole of the desk to behind it*)

Price-Hargraves. Miss Spencer, you've had a narrow escape.

Miss Spencer (*rising and gazing at Bloome*) Better luck next time.

Price-Hargraves. "Better luck . . . !" Miss Spencer, get me an aspirin.

Miss Spencer. Get 'em yourself—you eat too many. (*Leaning over Bloome's desk*) *You* never eat aspirins, do you, Mr Bloome? An aspirin to you—a daisy in a bull's mouth.

Price-Hargraves. Bull's—what are you talking about?

Miss Spencer (*to Price-Hargraves*) I wasn't talking to you—you're no bull. (*To Bloome, climbing on to the desk*) But to you!

Price-Hargraves. Miss Spencer, you're wanted.

Miss Spencer (*rapturously*) I know I am—and what a difference it makes!

Price-Hargraves. Lady Chesapeake is waiting for you.

Miss Spencer (*getting off the desk and moving to the door up* RC) Oh, what does the old cow want now?

Price-Hargraves. Old . . . ! Something to do with the prizes.

Miss Spencer. Damn the prizes. Stuff——

Price-Hargraves. What!

Miss Spencer. —and nonsense! (*To Bloome*) Be seeing you. It's *au revoir* but not good-bye, you beautiful, burgeoning, breath-taking Bloome!

(Miss Spencer *blows Bloome a stream of kisses and exits up* RC)

Price-Hargraves. Beautiful—what was the second word she used? It sounded terrible. And what have you done to her? You've transmogrified her—that's what you have done. And look at the shambles you've made of my office. (*Picking up a book from the floor*) Surely you didn't have time for reading?

Bloome. Miss Spencer just burst into the room. At the time I was on your desk with Miss Jones.

Price-Hargraves. On my desk! (*He runs below his desk and blots it with a semi-circular blotter*) I suppose Miss Jones was the *hors d'oeuvre*, and Miss Spencer the roast.

Bloome. All that happened is that we crawled from there to here . . .

Price-Hargraves. Before—or after?

Bloome. Both.

PRICE-HARGRAVES. Too weak to walk!

BLOOME. I had to hit her to stop her bawling. That's all that happened.

PRICE-HARGRAVES. But not all that happened on Wandsworth Common, eh?

BLOOME. Nothing happened on Wandsworth Common!

PRICE-HARGRAVES. We all know what happened on Wandsworth Common. On Wandsworth Common a girl was accosted, attacked, and, like any old peanut, assaulted.

BLOOME. But not by me.

PRICE-HARGRAVES. She's already identified you to the police.

BLOOME. If only I could persuade you.

PRICE-HARGRAVES. You can't persuade me any more than you'll persuade the judge. You'll be condemned and punished in court—and then you'll be condemned and punished here.

BLOOME. You can't be condemned and punished twice for the same offence.

PRICE-HARGRAVES. It's not the same offence. There's two offences.

BLOOME. What's the second one?

PRICE-HARGRAVES. Meggitts.

BLOOME. Maggots?

PRICE-HARGRAVES. Meggitts. (*He takes Bloome's order book from his desk drawer and moves down* C) Remember Lady Chesapeake's command about avoidable errors? You've made one, Bloome. A *monumental avoidable error*, Bloome, and you're not going to avoid a monumental punishment, Bloome.

BLOOME (*incredulously*) I made an error with Meggitts?

PRICE-HARGRAVES. You did. One hundred gross cartons of Chunkibix were ordered, and you only despatched one. When Lady Chesapeake hears about this you'll be fired, Bloome, fired, finished, flung out and forgotten.

BLOOME. Oh, my heavens. (*Moving* R *of Price-Hargraves*) Let me see. How did I make a mistake?

PRICE-HARGRAVES. How you did, doesn't matter. The point is, you *did*.

BLOOME (*frantically looking at the book*) I didn't!

PRICE-HARGRAVES. What do you mean?

BLOOME. *You* did. There's your initials.

PRICE-HARGRAVES. What! (*He scowls at the book and looks at it closely. Triumphantly*) So—you've been forging my signature!

BLOOME. No, no, look at the date. December the first. You always make me take my summer holidays then.

PRICE-HARGRAVES. There's only one way you can get yourself out of this mess. You can sign over my name.

BLOOME. But what if Lady Chesapeake should find out?

PRICE-HARGRAVES. There isn't a cat-in-hell's chance of her finding out.

(LADY CHESAPEAKE *sweeps in up* RC. *Over her gorgeous party dress she wears a high paper witch's hat*)

LADY CHESAPEAKE. What isn't there a cat-in-hell's chance of my finding out?

(PRICE-HARGRAVES *shoves the order book at Bloome and hastily moves away* LC)

Well, Mr Price-Hargraves, what were you just saying to Mr Bloome?
PRICE-HARGRAVES. I was just saying how you'd never know how much we loved you.
LADY CHESAPEAKE. That's very kind of you.
PRICE-HARGRAVES. We think you made a splendid old witch.
LADY CHESAPEAKE. Thank you. Now run along.

(BLOOME *moves behind the desk, puts the book away, and sits*)

PRICE-HARGRAVES. Run along?
LADY CHESAPEAKE. There's supposed to be a party going on—and there's no representative of Orders.
PRICE-HARGRAVES. Yes, of course. Mr Bloome can . . .
LADY CHESAPEAKE. Mr Bloome can stay put. One representative will suffice.
PRICE-HARGRAVES (*moving below her to the door*) Just as you say— but, I must say—my head . . .
LADY CHESAPEAKE (*scornfully*) Your head? And what about your head, Mr Price-Hargraves?
PRICE-HARGRAVES. Well, it's—it's in a whirl . . .
LADY CHESAPEAKE. Indeed, then kindly whirl it out of here.

(*Shaken to the core*, PRICE-HARGRAVES *exits*)

(*After watching Price-Hargraves' exit with contempt*) And how is *your* head, Mr Bloome?
BLOOME. Spinning. (*He swings in his chair away from her*)
LADY CHESAPEAKE. And your ears—are they burning? They should be—you are certainly being talked about. Your escapade on Wandsworth Common—as far as I can hear—seems to be the sole topic of conversation. Especially among the females. And I find their reaction to the affair most disturbing. Far from deploring what you have done, they . . . Mr Bloome!

(BLOOME *jumps and twists his chair towards her*)

I dislike intensely talking to a person's back. I should be loath to think that you were without morals *and* manners. Strange how one can be deceived. Never for one moment would I have taken you for a Casanova. When one thinks of such people—if one ever does—one thinks of them as being—well, not like you. Which leads me to wonder how many more wolves in sheep's clothing we are harbour ing in Chunkibix. Well, I must go. Are you coming to the prize giving?

BLOOME. I'd rather not, if you don't mind.

LADY CHESAPEAKE. Far from minding, I applaud your decision. It shows you do at least have some sensitivity. What do you propose to do?

BLOOME. Stay here out of the way.

LADY CHESAPEAKE (*moving to the door up* RC) Nonsense. You are staying till the end of the party, I presume?

BLOOME. As one of the organizers, there may be something . . .

LADY CHESAPEAKE. Quite. (*Casually, giving no hint of what she is going to say finally*) But you can't stay here. It's too cold. You'll go to my room. There's a fire, a settee, and a table with drinks. You may help yourself. (*With sudden complete change of tone*) I shall be along in ten minutes. (*She gives a diabolically naughty wink and exits*)

CURTAIN

SCENE 2

SCENE—*The same. Nine o'clock the following morning.*
　The room has been tidied up, but the decorations still remain in place. The flowers on the desk LC are very wilted and drooping in their vase.

When the CURTAIN *rises,* FIONA *is discovered sitting on Bloome's desk amongst a pile of autograph albums.* HAROLD *is lounging on Bloome's chair. They are both looking through the albums.*

FIONA (*reciting from the album*)
　　　　　　　　　"Roses are red.
　　　　　　　　　Violets are blue.
　　　　　　　　　Sugar is sweet,
　　　　　　　　　And so are you."

(*With a grimace*) Oooo!

HAROLD (*reciting from the album*)
　　　　　　　　　"Ain't it gorgeous,
　　　　　　　　　Ain't it bliss,
　　　　　　　　　I've signed the book,
　　　　　　　　　Now give us a kiss."

Cor! (*He throws the book on the desk in disgust*)

FIONA. Why didn't I bring mine? I will tomorrow.

HAROLD. Anybody'd think Cliff Richards was coming to work here. (*He takes a pile of letters to the desk* LC)

FIONA. Cliff! (*Scornfully*) Ooo, aren't you old hat!

(*Bloome's telephone rings*)

(*Into the receiver*) Good morning. Orders Department. Mr Bloome's secretary speaking.

(HAROLD *makes a face*)

. . . No, you can't, Cynthia. Anyway, he's not in yet. I've put your book third from the top . . . I'm sorry, but that's the best I can do. Now if you don't mind, we're very busy this morning. (*She replaces the receiver*) Really! Who do these girls from Despatch think they are?

Harold. You've all gone round the bend.

Fiona. But what a gorgeous bend! He's become famous, hasn't he? Here in Chunkibix, I mean.

Harold (*with a snort*) Famous! What as?

Fiona. A symbol.

Harold. A—symbol?

Fiona. Symbol of sex status! (*Rapturously*) Ooh, he's fab! Everybody says so.

Harold (*shortly*) I don't.

Fiona. Huh! You! He's the absolute fabbest. You should hear all the girls on about him. They could scratch my eyes out 'cos I work in his office, and they don't.

Harold (*beginning to lose his temper*) Now look, Fiona! (*He glances quickly round at the door up* RC, *then grabs Fiona to him and gives her a long, clumsy, lingering kiss*)

Fiona (*immediately after the kiss, which she takes as a complete matter of course*) I wonder if he'd give me a photograph if I asked him?

Harold (*breaking away* L; *fuming*) Oh!

Fiona. Ooo—if he would!

(Miss Spencer *enters up* RC. *She carries a large carrier-bag and wears a very "with it" coat and hat*)

Miss Spencer (*in something of a flutter*) 'Morning, Miss Jones.

Fiona. 'Morning, Miss Spencer. Enjoy the party last night?

Miss Spencer. Very much, thank you—oh, very much! Er—Mr Price-Hargraves not arrived yet, of course. 'Morning, Hopkins.

Harold. 'Morning, Miss Spencer.

Miss Spencer (*rather breathlessly*) Er—Mr—Mr Bloome isn't here either, is he?

Fiona (*with emotion*) Oooh, no! Not yet.

(Miss Spencer *puts the bag down by her desk.* Harold *gives a loud snort at Fiona's reaction*)

Miss Spencer. You got a cold, Hopkins? (*She removes her coat and hat*)

Harold. No, just a touch of nausea.

Miss Spencer. You should use a handkerchief. Have you sorted the letters? (*She comes down* C, *revealing a Carnaby Street mini-skirt outfit*)

Harold. Cripes! (*Quickly*) Yes, Miss Spencer.

Miss Spencer (*diving into the carrier-bag*) I want you to get me some water.

Harold (*with a resigned sigh*) Yes, Miss Spencer. (*He picks up ne small vase of flowers from the desk* LC)

Miss Spencer (*sharply*) What are you going to do with that?
Harold. Well, I thought you wanted me to . . .
Miss Spencer. Put that down.

(Harold *replaces the vase*)

(*Suddenly producing a long, ornate vase from the bag*) Fill this.
Harold (*taking the vase*) Yes, Miss Spencer.
Miss Spencer. And hurry.

(Harold *runs off down* r)

(*Moving to her own desk*) Have you dusted the desks, Miss Jones?
Fiona. I've done yours—and Mr Bloome's. I was just going to do
Mr Price-Hargraves. (*She moves to the desk* lc)
Miss Spencer. Well, get on with it. (*She dives into the bag again*)

(Fiona *dusts the desk* lc. Miss Spencer *produces an enormous autograph album with flowers on the cover. She goes to Bloome's desk, hiding
the book from Fiona*)

(*Seeing the other books*) What . . . ? (*Sharply*) What are these?
Fiona. They belong to a lot of the girls—the Mr Bloome Fan
Club.
Miss Spencer. Ridiculous! (*She hesitates a moment, undecided what
to do with her own autograph book, then hides it behind her back. Irritably*)
Haven't you finished with that desk yet?
Fiona. Give us a chance—I've only just started.
Miss Spencer. Oh, leave it!
Fiona (*gaping*) What? Leave Mr Price- . . .
Miss Spencer (*snapping*) We've no time for fiddling around this
morning. I gave you a letter to type just before we left last night.
Where is it?
Fiona. On my desk.
Miss Spencer. Get it. At once. Most important.
Fiona. Yes, Miss Spencer. (*Moving down* r) And when *he* comes in,
will you . . .
Miss Spencer. When *who* comes in?
Fiona (*her eyes on Bloome's desk; with a big sigh*) Him! Will you
tell him about the authograph books and ask him if he'd mind
signing 'em right away? The girls'll go mad if I don't get 'em done
by lunch time.

(Fiona *exits down* r. Miss Spencer *hesitates, then quickly scatters
the books on Bloome's desk in order to put hers on the most prominent
position. She then goes to her own desk.* Harold *enters down* r *with the
vase, now containing water. The telephone on the desk* lc *rings*)

Harold (*as he enters*) Here we are, Miss Spencer.
Miss Spencer (*moving quickly to the telephone*) Just a moment.

(Miss Spencer *sits at the desk* lc *to answer the telephone, not looking at Harold.* HAROLD, *during the conversation, puts the big vase on the desk* LC, *then moves to Bloome's desk, picks up Miss Spencer's autograph book casually, and looks through it, chuckling to himself at some of the things he reads*)

(*On the phone*) Orders here . . . Oh, put him through, will you? . . . Good morning, Mr Price-Hargraves' secretary speaking . . . No' I'm sorry, he's not here yet. Can I . . . ? Certainly . . . Yes . . . Yes . . . Oh, yes, I'll tell him. And you'll ring him—when did you say? . . . Three o'clock this afternoon . . . Yes, I'll make a note of it right away . . . Thank you. Good-bye. (*She replaces the receiver and begins writing on the note-pad*)

HAROLD (*as Miss Spencer replaces the telephone*) Cor! The muck people write in these things. Makes your tummy turn right over.

(MISS SPENCER, *busy writing, takes no notice*)

(*Turning a page*) Blimey! Just listen to this, Miss Spencer. (*Reading*)
             "Mildred sweet
             And Mildred fair;
             Mildred neat——

(MISS SPENCER *starts to take notice*)

             —Beyond compare.
             I can only gaze bewildered
             On the beauty of My Mildred!
             June, nineteen-forty."

(MISS SPENCER *glares stonily at Harold*)

HAROLD (*not looking at her; incredulously*) Did you *ever* in all your puff! And who the hell is Mildred, anyway? (*He turns quickly to the inside cover of the album and reads the name of the owner. He stiffens, closes the book slowly, puts it back on top of the pile, gulps hard, then slowly turns to face Miss Spencer. In a choking voice*) Er—will that be all, Miss Spencer?

MISS SPENCER (*ominously*) That *will* be all, Hopkins.

(HAROLD (*scuttles to the door up* RC, *turns, and gulps*)

HAROLD (*pointing to the vase*) The vase!

(HAROLD *shoots out through the door up* RC. *The moment he has gone* MISS SPENCER *rises, goes quickly to Bloome's desk and lovingly picks up her album. She speedily finds the page Harold was reading and gazes at it for a moment. She clutches it to her breast*)

MISS SPENCER (*mouthing inaudibly but dramatically, with her eyes closed*) I can only gaze *bewildered*—on the beauty of my Mildred. (*She shakes her head and sniffs emotionally*) June, nineteen . . . (*She breaks off, opens her eyes and looks at the page. Then she quickly picks up a pen from the desk and writes*) June, nineteen-*sixty*! (*She replaces the book on the pile, goes to her desk and bends over the carrier-bag. When she straightens up and turns she is holding four large, beautifully shaped chrysanthemums. She takes them to the desk* LC, *arranges them carefully in the big vase, then stands back to admire them. Suddenly she picks up the vase, and places it on Bloome's desk—again standing back to admire the flowers. She sniffs once more)*

(FIONA *enters down* R *with a newly typed letter and envelope.* MISS SPENCER *darts back to her own desk)*

FIONA (*moving up to Miss Spencer*) Here's the . . . (*She sees the flowers. Loudly and meaningly*) Oh! (*In her ordinary voice*) Here's the letter, Miss Spencer. (*She puts the letter on Miss Spencer's desk and turns to go, her eyes on the flowers)*

MISS SPENCER (*sharply*) Just a minute. I'd better check it. (*She reads the letter)*

FIONA. Fab, aren't they! (*She sniffs the flowers*) Lovely smell—like a graveyard!

MISS SPENCER (*still on the letter*) When I went to school . . .

FIONA. Coo—that's going back a bit, isn't it?

MISS SPENCER (*coldly and emphatically*) When I went to school . . .

FIONA (*pleasantly interested*) Expect things were a bit different then.

MISS SPENCER. Indeed they were—and a good thing too. Permissiveness was unknown in *my* schooldays.

FIONA. What? But what did you do when you wanted to go . . .

MISS SPENCER (*firmly*) And when I was at school the word "con firm" was spent C.O.N.F.I.R.M.

FIONA (*unabashed*) What have I put?

MISS SPENCER. C.O.N.F.*E*.R.M.

FIONA (*her eys again on the flowers; gaily*) Have I, really?

MISS SPENCER. You have.

FIONA. Oooh! Aren't I silly?

MISS SPENCER. You are. (*She glares at Fiona)*

FIONA (*her eyes on the flowers, her feet moving in the current dance step*) My mind must have been wandering. (*She gazes at Bloome's chair)*

MISS SPENCER (*coldly*) Has it returned? (*She reads again)*

FIONA. Not really. (*Sighing*) It's his fault, really. Blame him. (*Giggling*) Oooh! He's got a lot to answer for, hasn't he!

MISS SPENCER (*deliberately concentrating on the letter*) "Yours truly" —truly—T.R.E.W.L.Y. Well, really!

FIONA. Really and truly! I never put that, did I? (*With a happy laugh*) I'm not with it this morning, am I?

MISS SPENCER. You will kindly *get* with it when you re-type.

(HAROLD *enters up* RC *with an enormous pile of autograph books tucked under his chin)*

HAROLD. To hell with this for a lark!

MISS SPENCER. Hopkins!

HAROLD. "Hopkins" my Aunt Fanny. I came here as a junior clerk, and what am I? Runner to a ruddy fan club! (*He almost hurls the books on to Bloome's desk)*

MISS SPENCER (*with a shriek*) Mind those flowers!
FIONA (*looking at the albums, excitedly*) Oooh! Look at 'em! Look at 'em! Isn't it fab! Must be nearly every girl in the building.

(PRICE-HARGRAVES' *voice is heard roaring just outside the door up* RC)

PRICE-HARGRAVES (*off; roaring*) Come back there! Do you hear me? Come back!
HAROLD. What the heck's going on?

(*The door up* RC *bursts open and wild-looking* PRICE-HARGRAVES *enters. He is carrying what appears to be a large folded sheet of blank white paper in his hand*)

PRICE-HARGRAVES (*to Harold*) Out! (*To Fiona*) Out! (*To Miss Spencer*) Out!

(FIONA *and* HAROLD *dive for the door down* R, MISS SPENCER *crosses below Price-Hargraves towards the door up* RC)

(*Moving above his desk*) Wait! Wait! Wait!

(*The three stop dead in their tracks*)

Do any of you know anything about this? (*He holds the paper out, still folded*) Hopkins?
HAROLD. I don't know anything about anything this morning!
PRICE-HARGRAVES. Miss Jones?
FIONA. I don't know what you're talking about.
PRICE-HARGRAVES. Miss Spencer? (*Hastily*) Good heavens, no. You wouldn't. Now, I'll tell you. This filthy, dirty, slimy, bestial, obscene, pornographic notice—which I shall show you all in a minute!—has been pinned on our door—for all the world to see. What do you make of that, Miss Spencer? (*He holds up the paper for all to see*)
HAROLD (*reading it line by line*)
                SEX DEPARTMENT
                YOU WANT IT!
                WE SUPPLY IT!

(*There is a moment's silence, then* FIONA *and* HAROLD *go off into peals of laughter*)

PRICE-HARGRAVES (*roaring*) Silence!

(FIONA *and* HAROLD *stop laughing. Everyone looks at Miss Spencer*)

Well, Miss Spencer?

(MISS SPENCER *is standing transfixed, staring at the notice. She stands thus for quite a while, then begins to laugh, quietly at first, then louder until she becomes almost hysterical with mirth. The others gape at her unbelievingly.* MISS SPENCER *totters to the desk* LC *and collapses in Price-Hargraves' chair*)

FIONA (*goggling*) Well, would you . . . !
HAROLD. Stone the crows!

(FIONA *and* HAROLD *join Miss Spencer in laughing*)

PRICE-HARGRAVES (*clapping his hands frantically and shouting*)
Silence!

(*The laughter ceases*)

MISS SPENCER (*quietly, but with laughter in her voice*) "You want it—
we supply it."

(*Immediately the three go off into roars of laughter again.* PRICE-
HARGRAVES *begins* "Outing", *but no avail. He is so enraged he scarcely
realizes what he is doing. Little bursts of* "Take a week's notice"—
"Collect your cards"—"Fired, the lot of you" *come from him. In sheer
exasperation he moves below his desk, snatches the limp flowers from his
little vase, shoves them under Miss Spencer's nose as if they were smelling-
salts, then hurls them dramatically into the waste-paper basket under his
desk and stamps away* L)

HAROLD. Say it with flowers!

(*The laughter starts anew*)

PRICE-HARGRAVES. Unless this levity ceases . . . !

(*The laughter dies away, to be replaced by sniffs from* FIONA *as she dabs
her eyes, and groans of agony—the kind that follows a burst of laughter—
from Harold, who is holding his stomach and writhing*)

(*Topping the noise, in an attempt to restore order*) Miss Spencer, take a
letter. (*Dictating loudly*) Thompson Brothers, High Street, Chelms-
ford. "Dear Sirs," . . .

MISS SPENCER. "You want it. We supply it."

(FIONA *and* HAROLD *start laughing hysterically again*)

PRICE-HARGRAVES (*gibbering*) Miss—Miss *Spencer!* (*He screws up the
"notice", hurls it to the floor, then turns on Harold and Fiona*) Out! Out!

(FIONA *and* HAROLD *run out down* R)

Miss Spencer, I—(*gulping*)—I will give you five minutes to pull yourself together, and when I return I will be grateful if I may be
allowed to sit at my own desk! (*He stamps quickly to the door up* RC)

(*As Price-Hargraves reaches the door, it opens and* LADY CHESAPEAKE
enters. MISS SPENCER *rises and moves from the desk.* LADY CHESAPEAKE
is in great form, very different from her usual cold and austere self)

LADY CHESAPEAKE (*to Price-Hargraves*) What's this? What's this,
Mr Price-Hargraves? Are we absconding with the petty cash?
PRICE-HARGRAVES (*blinking*) I beg your pardon?

LADY CHESAPEAKE (*indicating his outdoor clothes with a gay wave*)
We appear to be dressed for a quick get-away, don't we?

PRICE-HARGRAVES. Get-away? I've only just got here.

LADY CHESAPEAKE (*with a trilling laugh*) Good heavens, man! I
was only joking.

PRICE-HARGRAVES (*with a shudder*) Joking? You—jo . . . (*He pulls
himself together with a little cough, and moves away* LC)

LADY CHESAPEAKE (*moving down* C) It would be a sorry world if
we couldn't have a little joke now and again, don't you agree?

PRICE-HARGRAVES (*wretchedly*) Yes, yes, indeed. (*As an after-
thought*) Ha, ha!

LADY CHESAPEAKE. I just called in to say how delighted I was
with the party. *Delighted*. (*To herself*) Most satisfactory. Truly a day
to remember. (*Again with her thoughts*) Yes, indeed. A *night* to remember.

PRICE-HARGRAVES. Thank you, Lady Chesapeake.

LADY CHESAPEAKE (*gaily*) Not at all! It is I who must thank *you*.
After all, most of the organization was done from this office, wasn't
it? I am greatly indebted to you, Mr Price-Hargraves, and, of course,
to Bernard.

(LADY CHESAPEAKE *has spoken the name quite naturally, entirely
unaware of the effect on* MISS SPENCER *and* PRICE-HARGRAVES, *whose
heads shoot up—they are unable to believe their ears*)

(*Looking round gaily*) Where is he?

MISS SPENCER. He—er—arranged to call on Watkins Limited on
the way to the office, Lady Chesapeake.

(PRICE-HARGRAVES *can only gape at ¨Lady Chesapeake, open-
mouthed*)

LADY CHESAPEAKE. Oh, I see.

(MISS SPENCER *moves to her own desk and stands by it*)

(*To Price-Hargraves*) Well, when he returns you *will* tell him how
grateful I am to him for everything—*everything* he did!

PRICE-HARGRAVES (*dazed*) Oh. Yes, Lady Chesapeake.

LADY CHESAPEAKE (*brightly*) That is all I wanted to say. I shall
be in my office all the morning, should he need me. (*She turns and
opens the door. To Price-Hargraves; gaily*) You *will* put the petty cash
back, won't you! (*She waves to them coyly; with much gaiety*) Toodle-oo!

(LADY CHESAPEAKE *sails happily out up* RC. PRICE-HARGRAVES
staggers dazedly C)

PRICE-HARGRAVES (*at length; his voice throbbing with disbelief*)
Bernard! She called him Bernard! (*Still unable to grasp*) Bernard!
Twenty-two years I've been with the firm—and never, never once
has she called me *Reginald*! (*He moves to the hatstand in a daze. Unconsciously he puts his bowler on his head, removes his coat and hangs it*

up, then, still wearing his hat, moves down stage. His eyes turn to Bloome's desk and, for the first time, he notices the autograph books. He picks one up and glances at it) What on earth . . . ? *(He picks up another, looks at it, then throws it on the desk. He then notices the chrysanthemums)* And . . . ! *(He looks at them, then slowly turns to Miss Spencer)*

*(*Miss Spencer *drops her eyes guiltily.* Price-Hargraves *moves to his own desk, slowly bends down, retrieves his own wilted bunch of flowers from the waste-paper basket, looks at them woefully for a moment, moves above the desk, puts the flowers in his small vase, and sits looking at them)*

(Suddenly slapping his hand noisily on the desk) I do not—repeat *not*—understand it!

Miss Spencer *(coldly)* What, Mr Price-Hargraves?

Price-Hargraves *(almost to himself)* These young flibberty-gibbets like Miss Jones—perhaps there's some excuse for them. But that Lady Chesapeake and you—you of all people, Miss Spencer—that *you* could behave in this way!

Miss Spencer *(moving to R of him)* You mean . . . ?

Price-Hargraves. A man chases a girl across a common with the worst possible motives in mind, and yet—far from condemning him—you and all the other females on the premises treat him as if he were some kind of—of hero.

Miss Spencer. Perhaps he is—to us.

Price-Hargraves *(gaping)* You stand there and tell me . . . ?

Miss Spencer. What I am telling you, Mr Price-Hargraves, is that I—and all the other *females*—in Chunkibix—are grateful to Mr Bloome.

Price-Hargraves. *Grateful?* For what, in heaven's name?

Miss Spencer *(giving every word its full value)* For proving to us that there is in this drab, dreary, benighted building, at least one man with red—hot—human—blood coursing through his veins, and not —repeat *not*—blue-black ink! *(Having got this out of her system, she turns and goes back to her desk, very happy)*

*(*Price-Hargraves *unconsciously tips his bowler back on his head a little and sits with his arms dangling loosely over the sides of his chair—out! There is a slight pause, then* Bloome *enters up* rc. *He is very confident and very happy. Also very smart, with a gardenia in the lapel of his coat. He wears the enormous dark glasses of the moment, and carries briefcase and umbrella)*

Bloome *(as he enters)* Good morning, Miss Spencer. 'Morning, P.H. *(Seeing the flowers)* Oh, daffodils, how lovely! Your idea, Miss Spencer?

*(*Bloome's *telephone rings)*

(Putting briefcase and umbrella on his desk and answering the telephone) Hello? . . . *(To the others)* It's the B.B.C.

Price-Hargraves *(aghast)* B.B.C.?

BLOOME. The Bernard Bloome Club. (*Into the receiver*) Oh, good! (*He rings off and turns to Price-Hargraves*) They say two more girls have joined the club. (*He puts his umbrella and bowler on the hatstand then moves briskly back to his desk and sits at it*)

(FIONA *enters down* R *and moves quickly to* C. *She is concealing a box of chocolates behind her back*)

FIONA (*as she enters*) 'Scuse me, I thought I heard . . . (*She sees Bloome and continues breathlessly*) I did! (*She moves above his desk to Bloome*) Oooh!

(BLOOME *removes his glasses and looks at* FIONA *pleasantly as she approaches very slowly, her eyes never leaving his face*)

BLOOME. Hi, Fi!
FIONA (*when she reaches very close to Bloome, bringing the opened box of chocolates into view; in a broken voice*) Have a choc!
BLOOME (*pleasantly*) Thank you. (*He takes one*)
FIONA (*pathetically*) Please—(*gulping*)—take two!
BLOOME (*taking another*) Thank you. (*He throws it up and catches it in his mouth*)
FIONA (*overcome*) Oooooooh!

(FIONA *turns and rushes blindly out of the room down* R)

BLOOME (*indicating the autograph books*) How I'm ever going to work with all this—er . . .
MISS SPENCER (*leaping gazelle-like across to Bloome's desk*) Let me, Mr. Bloome. (*She tidies the desk, putting the books on one corner*)
BLOOME. Thank you, Miss Spencer. How kind.

(MISS SPENCER *leans as close as she can to him as she works.* BLOOME *accepts such attentions with an easy, assured smile. With an effort,* PRICE-HARGRAVES *tries to pull himself together and, for the first time, moves a muscle.* MISS SPENCER *moves back to her desk*)

PRICE-HARGRAVES (*heavily*) Bloome . . .
BLOOME (*busy with his briefcase; politely, enquiringly*) P.H., dear fellow?
PRICE-HARGRAVES (*in a strangled croak*) Aaah!
BLOOME. Speak up, lad!
PRICE-HARGRAVES. Lady—Lady Chesapeake was asking . . .
BLOOME (*murmuring easily*) Ah yes—Clarissa . . .
PRICE-HARGRAVES. Clarissa! (*He staggers to his feet*)
BLOOME (*occupied*) What did she want?
PRICE-HARGRAVES (*putting his bowler on the hatstand and moving in anguish towards the door up* RC) Tell him, Miss Spencer—tell him. I feel—peculiar.

(HAROLD *enters up* RC)

HAROLD. 'Scuse me, but . . .

Price-Hargraves (*putting a hand on Harold's shoulder; weakly*)
Hopkins——

Harold. Sir?

Price-Hargraves. —take me to the canteen. I've had a traumatic experience.

Harold. Indeed, sir?

Price-Hargraves. I'm old and redundant.

Harold (*cheerfully*) You are, sir, aren't you.

Price-Hargraves. I think I'll have a large Ribena and soda.

(*Supported by* Harold, Price-Hargraves *exits up* RC. Harold *closes the door behind them*)

Bloome. Poor old P.H.—beginning to feel his age! (*Looking at some notes from his briefcase*) Oh, dear, these notes—I ought to get them—Miss Spencer, do you think Miss Jones could type these out for me? (*He rises*)

Miss Spencer (*decidedly*) No!

Bloome. I beg your pardon?

Miss Spencer. I will do them myself!

Bloome (*touched*) Oh—thank you, Miss Spencer.

Miss Spencer (*rising and taking her own autograph album to her bosom*) And, Mr Bloome—would you—could you? (*She opens the book at a blank page and places it in front of Bloome, if necessary sweeping any other autograph books out of the way*) In remembrance of—last night. (*Her hand goes to her cheek where Bloome struck her*)

Bloome (*willingly*) Of course, Miss Spencer—of course—*Mildred!*

(Miss Spencer *grabs the notes and runs to the door down* R)

Miss Spencer (*in a whisper*) Bernard!

(Miss Spencer *runs off down* R. Bloome *sits, preening himself, then picks up a pen and thinks of something to write. There is a knock on the door up* RC)

Bloome. Enter—enter! (*He concentrates on the book*)

(*The door opens slowly, and* Doris Povey's *head looks in. She looks at Bloome, who is intent on writing in the book*)

(*Without looking up*) How can I be of assistance to you?

Doris (*somewhat nervously*) Hullo!

(Bloome *looks round, then jumps up in a panic*)

Bloome. *You!*

Doris. Yes. Can I . . . ? (*She comes into the room, closing the door, and moves* C)

Bloome. No—no—you can't—how dare you! You mustn't . . .

Doris (*who is considerably more subdued than in the first act*) I had to see you, so I sneaked in.

Bloome (*still flustered*) But you shouldn't . . .

Doris. May I sit down? My feet are killing me. (*She sits* R *of the desk* LC *and puts her handbag on it*)

Bloome (*wildly*) Get out of here! If anyone . . .

Doris. But I had to come.

Bloome (*moving* C) Why?

Doris. Because it wasn't you.

Bloome. What?

Doris. It wasn't you. What went at me.

Bloome (*blankly*) Wasn't it? (*Suddenly*) Yes, it was. It must be!

Doris. I've seen him!

Bloome. Who?

Doris. The chap what went at me.

Bloome. But—but—you told the police . . .

Doris (*with a wail*) I know! I know! And honest, at the time I did think it was you, but the moment I saw this other fellow I knew it wasn't you. It was him.

Bloome. But . . .

Doris. I was having a cuppa coffee in a caff near Wandsworth Common and I suddenly noticed this fellow sitting at another table. The moment I saw him I recognized him, and I realized straight away I'd made a mistake when I'd said it was you who—ooh—I felt awful! But you can't blame me altogether. I mean, he was the spitten image of you really—same skinny shape, same skimpy hair, same funny nose——

(Bloome *feels his nose*)

—wearing exactly the same clothes as you. But it was his eyes—it was them that made me realize. They were quite different from yours. Oh, they were the same colour—but yours, well, they're sort of—well, not cod-fish *exactly*—but ——

Bloome. Thank you.

Doris. —but they're not what you'd call passionate, are they—not when you really come to look in 'em. They're more—mournful, and dopey—like those dogs you see in the adverts with brandy flasks round their necks. But this other chap—ooh!—they weren't just "get-up-them-stairs" eyes. They were "can't-wait-till-we-get-up-them-stairs eyes"—if you know what I mean.

Bloome. Quite—that is . . .

Doris. Well, when he went out of the caff I didn't know rightly what to do. But I made up my mind to come and see you straight-away—and here I am.

Bloome (*gloomily*) Yes—and I wish you weren't.

Doris. Well, I mean to say, it was the least I could do, wasn't it? When I think of the hell you must have been through the last couple of days—I had to come and release you from your purgatory at once. (*She starts to rise*)

Bloome (*pushing her back distractedly*) No! Stop—wait a moment . . .

Doris. Where's Aunt Mildred?

Bloome. Why?

Doris. I'm going to tell her the truth, of course. Go and find her quick.

Bloome (*suddenly*) No!

Doris. What?

Bloome. You're not going to say anything—not to the police—not to anybody!

Doris. But what about your purgatory?

Bloome. To h . . . I *like* my purgatory!

Doris. Are you dotty? You might land up in gaol.

Bloome. Not for a first offence. All I'll get is a ten-pound fine and a wink from the magistrate as I go out.

Doris. But I don't understand . . .

Bloome. You don't have to. All you have to do is keep your mouth shut.

Doris. But . . .

Bloome. Look, not a minute ago you said you've got to make up for your mistake, didn't you?

Doris. Yes, but . . .

Bloome. Well, here's your chance. Don't say a word.

Doris. But why—why?

Bloome (*shouting*) *Because!* That's why!

(Doris *stares at him, then strides to the door*)

Here—where . . . ?

Doris. I'm going to tell Aunt Mildred. I'm going to tell the truth. I'm going to save you in spite of yourself.

Bloome. I don't want to be saved in spite of myself! (*He takes her arm, and passes her across him to* c *again, earnestly*) Look, I don't suppose you'll understand, but I've been having the most wonderful time of my life. A whale of a time . . .

Doris. What? You mean because everybody thinks you went at me?

Bloome. Yes! Yes!

Doris (*getting angry*) Well, I like that! Nice friends you must have.

Bloome. So you see . . .

Doris. No, I don't see. (*Briskly*) And I'm off. To clear my conscience and save you from your purgatory. (*She grabs her bag, but it opens and the contents fall on the floor*) Oh damn! (*She kneels to pick them up*)

Bloome (*pleading*) Doris . . .

Doris. No.

Bloome. Doris!

Doris. No!

(Bloome *turns away in despair, muttering*)

(*Intent on picking up her things*) We've got to be saved, both of us.

Bloome (*half to himself*) If you knew how wonderful it's been. What a reputation I've got . . .

Doris. I think it's disgusting. But they must have been playing on your better self. (*She closes her bag and gets up. Looking at him*) You're a nice little man, really, you'll be glad when you feel clean again, when the stain of sin is washed away, and when you're not sailing under false pretences. (*She starts to the door*)

(*Doris's last words give* Bloome *a counsel of despair. He suddenly rushes at the door and tries to lock it*)

Bloome. Oh, of course, it doesn't lock. Blow it.

Doris (*backing slightly*) What's the matter now?

Bloome (*every inch the wolf*) So—(*he bares his teeth*) you thought it wasn't me, did you?

Doris. What?

Bloome (*with a terrible sneer*) Are you so sure?

Doris. What . . . ?

Bloome (*advancing on her with menace*) Are you so sure it wasn't me?

Doris. What?

Bloome. Look in my eyes—what do you see?

Doris. What?

Bloome (*irritably*) Stop saying what—what do you see?

Doris. Well, they squint a bit . . .

Bloome (*backing her* LC *below the desk*) How do you think I spend my evenings? Watching the telly? Not on your Nelly! Do you think you can repress nature for ever without something going bust? Aren't I a man with a man's devouring lust?

Doris. Coo, what a word to use!

Bloome (*suddenly grabbing her bag and throwing it aside*) Get over that desk!

Doris. You're bonkers.

Bloome (*tearing off his jacket*) Wasn't me, eh? (*He makes a quick jump and grabs her*) That was me, wasn't it?

(Doris *breaks away* L, *screaming*)

(*Chasing her down* L) This is going to be me again!

(Doris *dodges up* L *above the desk.* Bloome *follows her, seizing the telephone as he does so.* Doris *runs down* R *of the desk to* LC *again, to retrieve her handbag*)

(*Yelling into the telephone*) Get me the police—it was me! (*He slams down the receiver, runs to the door up* RC *and opens it. Shouting down the corridor*) I'm at it again! (*He gives a Tarzan cry*)

Doris (*running about down* LC) Help! I want Aunt Mildred! Help!

(Bloome *slams the door, runs to the screaming Doris and mildly slaps her face. Instantly she slaps him back, hard.* Bloome *falls flat on the floor*)

You brute!

(DORIS *tries to run over Bloome to the door, but trips over him. He scrambles up, grabs her, and pulls her back to the desk* LC. *As he bends her over it, trying to prevent her from running away,* PRICE-HARGRAVES *enters up* RC)

PRICE-HARGRAVES. Bloome! Not *again!*

(DORIS *breaks away and rushes out up* RC)

My poor desk.

(BLOOME *runs after* DORIS, *but she slams the door in his face.* PRICE-HARGRAVES *examines his desk and uses the blotter on it again.* BLOOME *picks up his jacket and puts it on, moving* C)

BLOOME. You know, P.H., you disappoint me.
PRICE-HARGRAVES. I—I . . . ?
BLOOME. I've always thought of you as a man of some—well—et's say not less than average intelligence.
PRICE-HARGRAVES (*bitterly*) Thank you, Bloome. (*He sits at his desk*)
BLOOME. But now you seem to be as dense as a November fog.
PRICE-HARGRAVES. Thank you again.
BLOOME. You were never able to see that I was assuming a character in this office. Putting on an act.
PRICE-HARGRAVES. Character? Act? I don't . . .
BLOOME. You thought me a harmless, necessary little man—well-behaved, inoffensive. Even now you imagine that what happened on Wandsworth Common was some sudden aberration—a hitherto unknown impulse of lust.
PRICE-HARGRAVES. Well, wasn't it?
BLOOME. Lust—yes! Unknown—no! Oh, no! You've never glimpsed the *other* Bernard Bloome. The one I've always managed to Hyde behind Jekyll—ha, ha!
PRICE-HARGRAVES. Hyde—Jekyll?
BLOOME. Bernard Bloome—sex-craved—sex-hungry—sex-devouring—sex of one and half a dozen of the other! I am possessed of a devil, Price-Hargraves—a devil!
PRICE-HARGRAVES. No, no!
BLOOME. Yes, yes! One hell of a devil. He courses through my body—(*illustrating graphically*)—here—(*touching his head*)—and—elsewhere. Even in the daytime his voice is never silent. But it is for the darkness of the night that he waits.
PRICE-HARGRAVES. At night-time you give in to this—er—devil?
BLOOME. I do not "give in" to him, Price-Hargraves. I glory in him. I welcome him with open—well, with open arms. The more evil he suggests, the more I welcome him.
PRICE-HARGRAVES. Good God!

Bloome. He urges me to look out of the window and see—see . . .
(*He pauses*)

Price-Hargraves (*getting interested*) See what?

Bloome. Wandsworth Common! And that great black void beckons to me with its promise of fleshy womanhood.

Price-Hargraves. Fleshy . . . ?

Bloome. Womanhood.

Price-Hargraves. That's how it was the other night?

Bloome. That's how it is *every* night.

Price-Hargraves (*incredulously*) What?

Bloome. Sometimes twice-nightly.

Price-Hargraves. Oh!

Bloome. And with matinees.

Price-Hargraves. Matinees as well! (*He stares at Bloome*)

(Bloome, *staring back, gives a short nod*)

(*Licking his lips slightly*) What—what happens?

Bloome (*suiting the action to the word*) I rush in pursuit of my lovely victim, every muscle and fibre of my being thrilling with the chase. (*He beats his breast in the manner of King Kong*)

(Price-Hargraves, *somewhat hypnotized, half copies Bloome's action*)

Price-Hargraves. Yes—yes?

Bloome. Her golden hair streams behind her—maddening me—see!

Price-Hargraves (*looking*) Yes—yes!

Bloome (*pointing elsewhere*) She's over there!

Price-Hargraves (*looking in the new direction*) Oh, yes, of course. Golden hair . . .

Bloome (*wrenching off a shoe and hurling it up stage*) A shoe flies off —her's, of course . . .

Price-Hargraves (*more and more carried away*) Of course!

Bloome (*moving* R *of his own desk*) I overtake her—I have her pinioned . . .

Price-Hargraves (*rising and moving to Bloome*) Pinioned—good heavens!

Bloome. Back and front . . .

Price-Hargraves. Back . . .

Bloome. And *then* . . .

Price-Hargraves (*wildly excited*) Then . . . ?

Bloome (*abruptly breaking the spell*) Mind your own business.

Price-Hargraves (*agonized*) But you can't stop there!

Bloome. I don't. (*He stares at Price-Hargraves*)

(Price-Hargraves *makes a "well, go on" gesture*)

(*Slowly*) Why do you want to know what happened then, Price-

Hargraves? (*Quickening*) Why did you want to know that? Shall I tell you?

Price-Hargraves (*backing above his desk*) No, no. I don't want to know.

Bloome (*following him*) But I want to know. Day after day I've watched you—watched those slow jellyfish eyes of yours begin to glitter and gleam . . .

Price-Hargraves. *My* jellyfish eyes?

Bloome. Yours, Price-Hargraves. Glitter and gleam, Price-Hargraves.

Price-Hargraves. But when do they . . . ?

Bloome. Whenever that girl, that Fiona, comes into the office. (*He picks up his shoe and quickly puts it on*)

Price-Hargraves (*completely horrified*) Miss Jones! (*He collapses into his chair*)

Bloome. To glitter, gleam and glow, Price-Hargroves. And *Glow!*

Price-Hargraves. I have *never* glowed at Miss Jones. I hate the wretched girl.

Bloome. You hate her because you can't possess her.

(Price-Hargraves *starts to protest*)

(*Topping him*) Yes, because you can't possess her! You *dirty* old man!

Price-Hargraves. Stop, stop, I beseech you!

Bloome. And what's more . . .

Price-Hargraves. There can't be more!

Bloome. There can—more and more.

Price-Hargraves. What? What?

Bloome (*fortissimo*) *Miss Spencer!*

Price-Hargraves (*in a whisper*) Miss Spencer! (*Brokenly*) This is too much.

Bloome. I should have thought so myself. But not you. All is grist that comes to your mill.

Price-Hargraves. I haven't got a mill.

Bloome. Haven't you? (*Suddenly*) Your hands, Price-Hargraves —your hands!

Price-Hargraves (*looking at his hands*) What's the matter with them?

Bloome. I've watched them. What do they do every time you see Miss Spencer turn her back on you? Those hands?

Price-Hargraves (*rising in a panic*) No, no!

Bloome (*deadly, every word separately pronounced*) They make to pat her imagined bottom.

Price-Hargraves. No, Bloome, you're wrong, you're wrong. Miss Spencer hasn't *got* a bottom.

Bloome. That's why I said "imagined". And why do you gleam, glitter, glow and pat, Price-Hargraves? Because—(*emphatically*)— you, too, have got a devil! (*He moves* r *of his own desk*)

Price-Hargraves. Have I?

BLOOME. In fact, Price-Hargraves, you're a hypocrite.

PRICE-HARGRAVES (*moving above the chair* R *of his desk*) A hyp . . .

BLOOME. A hippie-hypocrite! Can you truly point a finger at me? Can you point *anything* at me?

PRICE-HARGRAVES. Well . . .

BLOOME. Have *you* never done anything of which you are ashamed?

PRICE-HARGRAVES. Never.

BLOOME. Never pinched a sexy poster from the Underground?

PRICE-HARGRAVES. Never!

BLOOME. Never drawn a moustache on a girl's . . .

PRICE-HARGRAVES. Never!

BLOOME. Never written rude words on the wall at school?

PRICE-HARGRAVES. Never!

BLOOME. On the blackboard?

PRICE-HARGRAVES. Nev . . . (*He breaks off, horrified*) How did you know?

BLOOME. Ha! What was the rude word?

PRICE-HARGRAVES. I shan't tell you.

BLOOME. *What was the rude word you wrote on the blackboard?*

PRICE-HARGRAVES (*weakening*) I shan't . . .

BLOOME (*relentlessly*) What was the word!

(*There is an agonized pause, then* PRICE-HARGRAVES *bursts out with his confession*)

PRICE-HARGRAVES (*desperately*) French knickers!

(BLOOME *takes a step back in apparent triumphant horror*)

Now that you know, why shouldn't the whole world know? (*He rushes to the door up* RC *and shouts*) French knickers! (*He runs back to his own desk, picks up both telephones and yells*) French knickers! (*He moves down* L *of his desk*)

BLOOME (*picking up his telephone*) Calling International Rescue! (*Advancing on Price-Hargraves again*) When you wrote French knickers on the blackboard, you imagined somebody wearing them, didn't you? Who was it?

PRICE-HARGRAVES. I'm not going to tell you.

BLOOME (*browbeating him*) When you wrote French knickers on the blackboard, who in your steaming imagination was wearing them? Some film star? The matron? Who was it?

PRICE-HARGRAVES (*with a cry of anguish*) The headmaster!

BLOOME (*drawing back*) A man?

PRICE-HARGRAVES. Of course he was a man. But I didn't know the difference between men and women then. (*Brokenly*) I was only nineteen!

BLOOME (*backing Price-Hargraves down* L) So you see, you too have a devil.

PRICE-HARGRAVES. A devil like yours?

BLOOME. Not like mine. (*He stands* LC *and draws himself up proudly to his full height, with his hands above his head pointing outwards to resemble the horns of a bull*) Mine is the Bull of Wandsworth Common!

(LADY CHESAPEAKE *marches in up* RC)

LADY CHESAPEAKE (*speaking to those following her*) Come in, all of you.

(FIONA, DORIS, HAROLD *and* MISS SPENCER, *in that order, enter up* RC. *They file past Lady Chesapeake and form a diagonal line behind Bloome's desk to down* R)

You've got to hear the truth—the whole truth! (*Pointing at Bloome*) The truth about that man.

(BLOOME'S "*horns*" *begin to droop downwards*)

He *didn't* do it.

(BLOOME'S *hands drop to his sides and he tries to sneak away, crossing below Price-Hargraves to down* L)

(*Instantly*) Come back!

PRICE-HARGRAVES (*moving* LC) What didn't he do?

LADY CHESAPEAKE. Did not attack Miss Spencer's niece on Wandsworth Common. The girl has just been to me. (*To Doris*) Haven't you!

DORIS. Yes. (*She glares at Bloome*)

(*There is an appalled silence.* BLOOME *wilts and shrinks*)

PRICE-HARGRAVES (*thunderously*) So you didn't do it!

BLOOME (*in his old, subjugated tone*) P.H. . . .

PRICE-HARGRAVES (*bullying*) Don't P.H. me! It's Mr Price-Hargraves from now on! Giving me all that twaddle about fleshy womanhood! You've never seen any fleshy womanhood in your life. And making me admit about the French knickers . . . (*Hastily turning to Lady Chesapeake*) Oh, I'm sorry, Lady Chesapeake. I wasn't talking about you—I mean, I wasn't suggesting you knew anything about French knickers—that is—I really don't know what I'm suggesting. You've no idea of the state I'm in.

LADY CHESAPEAKE (*coldly*) In? Unless normal service is resumed in this office in ten minutes, you are *OUT*!

(LADY CHESAPEAKE *sweeps out up* RC. FIONA, DORIS *and* HAROLD *all exit down* R, *their noses well in the air.* MISS SPENCER *moves up* C. BLOOME *and* PRICE-HARGRAVES *move dejectedly to their respective desks and sit*)

PRICE-HARGRAVES. Miss . . .

MISS SPENCER. Mr Price-Hargraves, I wish to give a week's notice.

PRICE-HARGRAVES. A week's notice, Miss Spencer? Why?

Miss Spencer (*moving down* R) Because in future I wish to work in an office where men are men, and not—repeat *not*—(*turning in the doorway down* R) maggots and *mice!*

(Miss Spencer *exits down* R, *slamming the door*)

Price-Hargraves. Me, a maggot?
Bloome. Me, a mouse?

(*After a moment's pause,* Price-Hargraves *suddenly leaps up, grabs his own and Bloome's bowlers from the hatstand, and moves to the door up* RC)

Price-Hargraves. Come on, Bloome! (*He throws Bloome's hat to him*)
Bloome (*rising and quickly following him*) Where are we going?
Price-Hargraves (*opening the door*) Where do you think? *Wandsworth-bloody-Common!*

Price-Hargraves *and* Bloome *rush through the doorway up* RC *together, as—*

the Curtain *falls*

FURNITURE AND PROPERTY LIST

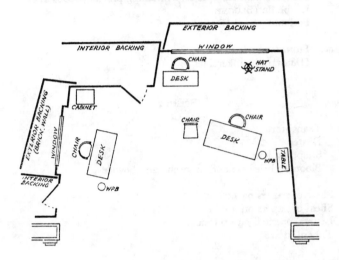

ACT I

SCENE I

On stage: Large ornate desk (LC) *On it:* writing materials, hand blotter,
2 telephones, paper-knife, note-pads, books, In and Out
trays, papers, small vase of flowers, bowl of paper-clips,
rubber. L *of it:* waste-paper basket

Smaller desk (R) *On it:* writing materials, hand blotter, blotting
paper, telephone, note-pads, bowl of paper-clips. *Below it:*
waste-paper basket. *In upstage drawer:* order book. *In downstage
drawer:* loose papers

Secretary's desk (up C) *On it:* typewriter, note-pads, papers,
writing materials

Table (L) *On it:* telephone directories, books, files

Filing cabinet (up R) *On it:* pencil sharpener, files

Hatstand (up C)

3 desk chairs

1 small chair (R of large desk)

On walls: advertisement posters (Chunkibix), etc.

Carpet

Off stage :   Duster (FIONA)
            Bag containing transistor radio, compact, lipstick (FIONA)
            Folder of letters (HAROLD)
            Shopping bag containing bunch of flowers (MISS SPENCER)
            Water for vase (HAROLD)
            Briefcase and umbrella (PRICE-HARGRAVES)
            Briefcase with zip opener, containing papers (BLOOME)
            Umbrella (BLOOME)
            Pad and pencil (FIONA)

Personal :   FIONA: watch
            HAROLD: handkerchief

SCENE 2

Strike :   Transistor
         Duster
         Shopping bag
         Bloome's briefcase and umbrella and bowler

Set :   Sheaf of papers on LC desk
       Sheaf of papers on R desk
       Letters, opened, on up C desk
       Tidy all desks

Off stage :   2 ledgers (HAROLD)

Personal :   PRICE-HARGRAVES: watch

ACT II

SCENE 1

Strike :   Ledgers
         Everything from hatstand

Check :   Order book in R desk drawer

Set :   Balloons (one prepared with pinpricks), paper trumpet and small
       adding machine on R desk
       Whisky bottle and glass in downstage cupboard of LC desk
       Pint tumbler in upstage drawer of R desk
       Christmas decorations all around room
       Tidy desks

Personal: BLOOME: paper hat
HAROLD: paper hat
PRICE-HARGRAVES: paper hat
LADY CHESAPEAKE: paper hat (witch)
MISS SPENCER: hat (fez)
FIONA: paper hat

SCENE 2

Strike: Balloons, trumpet and adding machine from R desk

Set: Large pile of autograph books on R desk
Duster on R desk
Replace articles from floor to LC desk
Tidy desks

Off stage: Carrier bag containing 4 chrysanthemums, large autograph album, ornate vase (MISS SPENCER)
Letter and envelope (FIONA)
Pile of autograph albums (HAROLD)
Large sheet of paper with notice (PRICE-HARGRAVES)
Briefcase and umbrella (PRICE-HARGRAVES)
Briefcase containing notes, and umbrella (BLOOME)
Box of chocolates, open (FIONA)

Personal: BLOOME: gardenia, dark glasses
DORIS: handbag full of cosmetic articles, etc.

LIGHTING PLOT

Property fittings required: 2 pendants
    Interior. An office. The same scene throughout
    THE APPARENT SOURCES OF LIGHT are: by day, windows R and up C;
      by night, 2 pendants
    THE MAIN ACTING AREAS are R, up RC, down RC, down C, LC

ACT I, SCENE 1. Morning
To open: Effect of bright winter daylight
No cues

ACT I, SCENE 2. Morning
To open: As previous scene
No cues

ACT II, SCENE 1. Midnight
To open: Pendants on. Blue in window floods
No cues

ACT II, SCENE 2. Morning
To open: As Act I
No cues

EFFECTS PLOT

ACT I

Scene 1

Scene 2

ACT II

Scene 1

MADE AND PRINTED IN GREAT BRITAIN BY
LATIMER TREND & COMPANY LTD PLYMOUTH

MADE IN ENGLAND